DANIEL EXPLAINED

DANIEL Explained

Charles R. Thompson

Daniel Explained
Copyright © 2018 by Charles R. Thompson
Tisip Company
Wesley Chapel, FL 33543

All scripture quotations are from the *King James Version* of the Bible unless otherwise indicated.

Printed in the United States of America
ISBN 978–0-9833869–9-5
Library of Congress Control Number: 2018913371

CONTENTS

Appendices

ACKNOWLEDGMENTS

I would like to express special thanks to my wife Sandra Thompson, who has always been there standing by my side. Her encouragement, consistent prayers of wisdom, knowledge, and fortitude, caused me to overcome many obstacles. Her loving attitude of enthusiasm and spiritual assertiveness has generated and stimulated a prolonged and lasting marriage. She sacrificed many hours of quality time, but her lack of selfishness brought about a transformation of love and respect drawing us nearer to God and closer to each other. Thank you, my dear!

I would like to thank my children, family, friends, and love-ones for enduring some of the early Bible studies. They donated many pain-staking hours of their time as my initial audience as I presented this information to them. They listened intently, and they challenged me for more details. Their continual support enabled me to develop a more thorough skillset; thereby stimulating hunger and thirst for more of the word of God.

Preface

WHEN referencing the book of Daniel, most people think about the challenges Daniel and his friends endured. Our sympathy goes out to them. Daniel spent the night in the den of hungry lions. Shadrach, Meshach, and Abednego shared a time of fellowship in the fiery furnace. Still, others are reminded of Daniel's Seventieth Week, a reference to God's timeline in dealing with the Hebrew people. The book of Daniel is much more than stories of faith and endurance. It is about the life of a young man who was exiled from his homeland and the challenges he faced as he continued to serve his God.

After his exile, he underwent several drastic changes in his life. His captors changed his name. They changed his diet. Everything that he knew and understood became inverted in an instant. While in exile, he was catapulted into the upper echelons of society. His fame was both victorious and notorious. He was victorious because he obeyed the words of the Lord, and he was notorious because the Lord's favor promoted him quicker than his local counterparts. Through it all, he maintained his obedience to God's word, and he received blessings for it beyond measure.

The book of Daniel's primary focus is on the events of the latter days. It consists of a series of dreams and visions that correspond to past events and events that are still future today. It is a roadmap that reveals the kingdoms of the past and kingdoms that are yet to come. Daniel wrote this book in a foreign country, while he was being held captive in Babylon. Daniel's gifting was in interpreting dreams and visions, and he utilized his gift several times. Each dream, whether it was his dream or the dream of another, was always associated with prophecy and other end-time events. Even though he was an interpreter of dreams, there were some dreams,

visions, and revelations that even he needed assistance in acquiring a mean-
ingful understanding. One of the critical facets of the book of Daniel is
that no matter what obstacles or challenges he encountered, he remained
faithful to his God.

Daniel exercised his gifts to enhance the understandings of dignitaries
and to provide prophetic insight to future generations. He always operated
within the boundaries set by the Lord. Before taking any action, Daniel
always sought the Lord first, through prayer and supplication. He never
used his gift for gain, although the Lord blessed him far above expectation.
Even though Daniel spent most of his life in a strange land, he continued
to be obedient to the word of the Lord without wavering.

Taking the journey through this book will reveal some truths about
the different dreams and how they have a direct relationship with world
history, both past and future. It addresses some of the spiritual dynamics
that accompany true faithfulness. This book will enhance one's knowledge
of world history and better equip them with understanding the parallels
associated with Bible prophecy.

CHAPTER 1

THE BABYLONIAN CAPTIVITY

Dan. 1:1 In the third year of the reign of Jehoiakim king of Judah came Nebuchadnezzar king of Babylon unto Jerusalem, and besieged it.

Dan. 1:2 And the Lord gave Jehoiakim king of Judah into his hand, with part of the vessels of the house of God: which he carried into the land of Shinar to the house of his god; and he brought the vessels into the treasure house of his god.

The Fall of Judah

JEHOIAKIM was one of the kings of Judah. He was the son of King Josiah. He began his reign when he was twenty-five years old and reigned for eleven years in Judah. He was an evil king.

About the eighth year of Jehoiakim's reign, King Nebuchadnezzar of Babylon came against him and placed Judah under siege for three years. During the third year of the attack, King Nebuchadnezzar invaded the city of Jerusalem. He captured Jehoiakim, and he also took some of the holy vessels from God's temple and carried them back to Babylon. He found a new home for the sacred vessels that he confiscated from Jerusalem, storing them in the same house where he housed all of his Babylonian gods.

The Captives of Judah

Dan. 1:3   And the king spake unto Ashpenaz the master of his
            eunuchs, that he should bring certain of the children of
            Israel, and of the king's seed, and of the princes;

Dan. 1:4   Children in whom was no blemish, but well favoured,
            and skilful in all wisdom, and cunning in knowledge, and
            understanding science, and such as had ability in them
            to stand in the king's palace, and whom they might teach
            the learning and the tongue of the Chaldeans.

A man named Ashpenaz was the master of the eunuchs. Please note, a eunuch is not necessarily a male person that has undergone castration. Often in scripture, a eunuch is referring to an officer in the military. Ashpenaz was master of the eunuchs; therefore, he held a high-ranking military position with many subordinates under his authority.

Nebuchadnezzar commanded Ashpanaz to bring specific individuals back to Babylon. The king's list included King Jehoiakim's children, high-ranking governmental officials, and other gifted and talented individuals that are cunning in knowledge, skillful in wisdom, and possess an understanding of the sciences. No captive could have any blemishes or handicaps, and they must possess the ability to stand in the king's palaces, and are capable of learning the language of the Chaldeans.

Dan. 1:5   And the king appointed them a daily provision of the
            king's meat, and of the wine which he drank: so nour-
            ishing them three years, that at the end thereof they
            might stand before the king.

Dan. 1:6   Now among these were of the children of Judah,
            Daniel, Hananiah, Mishael, and Azariah:

Dan. 1:7   Unto whom the prince of the eunuchs gave names: for
            he gave unto Daniel the name of Belteshazzar; and to
            Hananiah, of Shadrach; and to Mishael, of Meshach;
            and to Azariah, of Abednego.

Ashpenaz brought many children of Judah back to Babylon, but the main focus is on Daniel, Hananiah, Mishael, and Azariah. The names of these men were changed to Babylonian names to eliminate any resemblance of their Hebrew heritage. They changed Daniel's name to Belteshazzar; Hananiah changed to Shadrach; Mishael changed to Meshach, and Azariah changed to Abednego.

Please note, all biblical names have specific meanings. Daniel's name means *God is my judge*.[1] The Babylonians changed his name to Belteshazzar, which means the *treasure of Bel*.[2] Hananiah's name means *the Lord is gracious*.[3] They changed his name to Shadrach, which means *command of God*.[4] Mishael's name means *who is or what God is*,[5] and they changed his name to Meshach, which means *he who belongs to Sheshach*,[6] which is a Babylonian king. Azariah's name means *the Lord has helped*,[7] and they changed his name to Abednego, which means *servant of Nebo*[8], a Babylonian deity. Upon closer examination of these new names, all of them have an association to either a Babylonian king or a Babylonian god.

King Nebuchadnezzar also appointed the Hebrew captives a special diet. He wanted them to abandon their Hebrew diet and eat Babylonian food that included drinking wine. He wanted them to be on the Babylonian menu for a minimum of three years. The king did not want to see the Hebrew children with any resemblance of their Hebrew heritage; including

---

[1] *The Nelson's New Illustrated Bible Dictionary* (Thomas Nelson Publishers, 1995), 326

[2] *Adam Clarke's Commentary on the Bible* (computer version) Dan. 1:7

[3] *The Nelson's New Illustrated Bible Dictionary* (Thomas Nelson Publishers, 1995), 538

[4] *The Nelson's New Illustrated Bible Dictionary* (Thomas Nelson Publishers, 1995), 1153

[5] *The Nelson's New Illustrated Bible Dictionary* (Thomas Nelson Publishers, 1995), 849

[6] *Adam Clarke's Commentary on the Bible* (computer version) Dan. 1:7

[7] *The Nelson's New Illustrated Bible Dictionary* (Thomas Nelson Publishers, 1995), 142

[8] *The Nelson's New Illustrated Bible Dictionary* (Thomas Nelson Publishers, 1995), 3

appearance, clothing, or speech. The king placed a time limit of a minimum of three years before any of the Hebrew children could appear before him.

> Dan. 1:8   But Daniel purposed in his heart that he would not defile himself with the portion of the king's meat, nor with the wine which he drank: therefore he requested of the prince of the eunuchs that he might not defile himself.
>
> Dan. 1:9   Now God had brought Daniel into favour and tender love with the prince of the eunuchs.
>
> Dan. 1:10 And the prince of the eunuchs said unto Daniel, I fear my lord the king, who hath appointed your meat and your drink: for why should he see your faces worse liking than the children which are of your sort? then shall ye make me endanger my head to the king.

Daniel was of Hebraic descent, and there were certain foods he was forbidden to eat. The consumption of certain foods would defile him (Lev. 11:1–47). Daniel purposed in his heart that he would not defile himself by partaking in certain portions of the king's diet; nor would he drink the king's wine. Perhaps Daniel had read the letter from Jeremiah, asking the captives to humble themselves (Jer. 29:1–7). Scripture does not say, whether or not the Babylonian food violated God's diet or whether or not the Babylonian food was sacrificial to idols. Whatever the reason, Daniel requested to be exempt from eating the king's food.

God gave Daniel favor with Ashpenaz; therefore Daniel spoke directly to him. He explained to him that eating the king's diet would cause him to defile himself. Daniel requested to be exempt from eating the king's diet. He asked that he be granted permission only to eat food approved by his God. Asphenaz refused to deviate from the king's commandment because to honor Daniel's request would be violating a direct order. He feared that if Daniel and company did not follow the king's diet, they would not look as healthy as the other Hebrew children. That could lead to his execution for failure to obey orders. Ashpenaz liked Daniel a lot, but he feared King Nebuchadnezzar more.

Dan. 1:11   Then said Daniel to Melzar, whom the prince of the eunuchs had set over Daniel, Hananiah, Mishael, and Azariah,

Dan. 1:12   Prove thy servants, I beseech thee, ten days; and let them give us pulse to eat, and water to drink.

Dan. 1:13   Then let our countenances be looked upon before thee, and the countenance of the children that eat of the portion of the king's meat: and as thou seest, deal with thy servants.

Dan. 1:14   So he consented to them in this matter, and proved them ten days.

After Asphenaz refused Daniel's request to change his diet, Daniel then turned to Melzar. Perhaps Melzar was Daniel's immediate supervisor. He challenged Melzar to prove one way or the other whether or not the Hebrew food will make them unhealthy. He reminded Melzar that the Hebrew diet is what caused them to be chosen to come to Babylon in the first place because their appearance was the best of the best.

Daniel's proposal to Melzar was to let them eat his natural diet for only ten days. The Hebrew diet consisted of water and pulse (vegetables). After ten days, he could compare their countenance to the appearance of those who were partaking of the king's food. If their debut was better than or equal to those eating the king's diet, then he could let them continue to feed them the Hebrew diet on a daily basis. Melzar thought that was a fair analysis; therefore, he decided to allow Daniel and friends to eat their native food for ten days.

Dan. 1:15   And at the end of ten days their countenances appeared fairer and fatter in flesh than all the children which did eat the portion of the king's meat.

Dan. 1:16   Thus Melzar took away the portion of their meat, and
             the wine that they should drink; and gave them pulse.
Dan. 1:17   As for these four children, God gave them knowledge
             and skill in all learning and wisdom: and Daniel had
             understanding in all visions and dreams.

After ten days of eating only the Hebrew diet, Daniel and friends appeared healthier than all the other captives that were partaking of the king's food. The fact that they looked more robust than their counterparts is a direct reflection of the importance of God's diet versus man's diet. Melzar quickly changed Daniel and his friend's menu from the king's food to the Hebrew diet, and they partook of the Hebrew diet for three years. Not only was their appearance better than their counterparts, but their menu also provisioned them with knowledge and skill in all wisdom and learning. Daniel specialized in understanding visions and dreams.

Dan. 1:18   Now at the end of the days that the king had said he
             should bring them in, then the prince of the eunuchs
             brought them in before Nebuchadnezzar.
Dan. 1:19   And the king communed with them; and among them
             all was found none like Daniel, Hananiah, Mishael, and
             Azariah: therefore stood they before the king.
Dan. 1:20   And in all matters of wisdom and understanding, that
             the king inquired of them, he found them ten times
             better than all the magicians and astrologers that were in
             all his realm.
Dan. 1:21   And Daniel continued even unto the first year of king
             Cyrus.

At the end of the three years of eating the Hebrew's diet, Ashpenaz presented Daniel and company before King Nebuchadnezzar. The king talked with Daniel and company and determined that they were the brightest and smartest of all the Hebrew captives brought from Jerusalem.

The king was impressed because they were ten times better than all the Babylonian magicians and astrologers. Daniel and company were promoted to be rulers over the whole province of Babylon (Dan. 2:48–49).

Daniel served as interim leader for the remainder of the Babylonian kingdom. Daniel was deposed from his position, after the overthrow of the Babylonian kingdom by the Medo-Persians, under the reign of King Cyrus. Although he was relieved of his duties, the new regime continued to hold him captive.

Daniel also served under another king named Darius. There he also received a promotion to a new position. Daniel was promoted to first president over one hundred and twenty princes and two presidents (Dan. 6:1–2). There's no definitive proof that Daniel ever returned to Jerusalem, but there was a man named Daniel that returned to Jerusalem with Ezra in the second exodus from Babylonian captivity (Ezr. 8:1–2). It's possible this is Daniel, but scripture does not confirm it.

CHAPTER 2

THE KING'S DREAM

Dan. 2:1   And in the second year of the reign of Nebuchadnezzar
            Nebuchadnezzar dreamed dreams, wherewith his spirit
            was troubled, and his sleep brake from him.
Dan. 2:2   Then the king commanded to call the magicians, and
            the astrologers, and the sorcerers, and the Chaldeans,
            for to shew the king his dreams. So they came and stood
            before the king.
Dan. 2:3   And the king said unto them, I have dreamed a dream,
            and my spirit was troubled to know the dream.
Dan. 2:4   Then spake the Chaldeans to the king in Syriack, O king,
            live for ever: tell thy servants the dream, and we will
            shew the interpretation.

The Nightmare

IN the second year of the reign of King Nebuchadnezzar, the king had a dream. Perhaps it was a nightmare because it woke him up. To make matters worse, he could not remember the contents of the dream. King Nebuchadnezzar commanded all the wise men to come to his office at once. As per their job description, they stood ready to listen to the king's dream and then provide the king with its interpretation. Note, the vision frightened King Nebuchadnezzar so much that he could not remember the dream's contents. This time, he had an unusual request for them. He began by requesting the wise men reveal to him the contents of his vision.

At this point, the wise men were unaware that the king did not remember his dream. All they knew is that the king's vision frightened him.

They stood ready, waiting for the king to reveal the dream's contents, but he never did because he could not remember it. Finally, they requested the king to disclose the contents to them, so they could reveal its interpretation.

Dan. 2:5   The king answered and said to the Chaldeans, The thing is gone from me: if ye will not make known unto me the dream, with the interpretation thereof, ye shall be cut in pieces, and your houses shall be made a dunghill.

Dan. 2:6   But if ye shew the dream, and the interpretation thereof, ye shall receive of me gifts and rewards and great honour: therefore shew me the dream, and the interpretation thereof.

When the wise men asked King Nebuchadnezzar to tell them the dream, he informed them that he had forgotten it. His request was remarkable because he demanded that they reveal to him the vision and its interpretation. He threatened the wise men that if they could not explain the dream and then provide its meaning, then they would be cut into pieces and their houses would become dunghills. On the other hand, if they revealed the vision and its understanding, they would receive gifts, rewards, and great honor. In other words, if they disclose to him the dream and the analysis, they would live, but if they did not reveal to him the vision and interpretation, they would die. It was an offer that they could not refuse.

Dan. 2:7   They answered again and said, Let the king tell his servants the dream, and we will shew the interpretation of it.

Dan. 2:8   The king answered and said, I know of certainty that ye would gain the time, because ye see the thing is gone from me.

Dan. 2:9   But if ye will not make known unto me the dream, there is but one decree for you: for ye have prepared lying and corrupt words to speak before me, till the time be

changed: therefore tell me the dream, and I shall know
that ye can shew me the interpretation thereof.

The wise men requested again that the king give them the dream,
and they would interpret it for him. The king informed the wise men that
he knew they were stalling because they knew he did not remember the
dream's contents. Then he reminded them that if they decide to lie to him
to save their lives; there would be only one outcome—*death*! If they could
not reveal the dream, then that would be confirmation that they were lying
about any interpretation they might attempt to impart to him.

Dan. 2:10   The Chaldeans answered before the king, and said,
              There is not a man upon the earth that can shew the
              king's matter: therefore there is no king, lord, nor ruler,
              that asked such things at any magician, or astrologer, or
              Chaldean.
Dan. 2:11   And it is a rare thing that the king requireth, and there is
              none other that can shew it before the king, except the
              gods, whose dwelling is not with flesh.

The wise men again reminded the king, there is not a man on earth
that could reveal the king's dream. The king's request was unprecedented;
no king, lord, or ruler, had ever requested such things of any magician,
astrologer, or Chaldean. The king's request was beyond the realm of possi-
bility. No other entity could fulfill such a request, except the gods that dwell
in the spiritual world. Note: the wise men were acknowledging that there is
a God in heaven, although they did not serve him.

Dan. 2:12   For this cause the king was angry and very furious, and
              commanded to destroy all the wise men of Babylon.
Dan. 2:13   And the decree went forth that the wise men should be
              slain; and they sought Daniel and his fellows to be slain.

The king was furious because the wise men could not reproduce his dream and the interpretation; therefore the king decided to issue an executive order. He decreed the execution of all of the wise men, without delay. This decree included Daniel and his friends, even though they were not present.

Dan. 2:14   Then Daniel answered with counsel and wisdom to Arioch the captain of the king's guard, which was gone forth to slay the wise men of Babylon:

Dan. 2:15   He answered and said to Arioch the king's captain, Why is the decree so hasty from the king? Then Arioch made the thing known to Daniel.

Dan. 2:16   Then Daniel went in, and desired of the king that he would give him time, and that he would shew the king the interpretation.

Arioch was captain of the king's guard, and he ordered his soldiers to carry out the executions of the wise men. Daniel, using his wisdom, asked Arioch, what is the accusation against them and what is the urgency for their punishment? Arioch explained the situation to Daniel. The king had a dream, but he could not remember the vision. Now he's demanding that the wise men reveal to him the contents of his nightmare and its interpretation.

Daniel took it upon himself to approach the king. He requested that if the king awards him a little more time, then he would disclose the king's dream and its interpretation.

Dan. 2:17   Then Daniel went to his house, and made the thing known to Hananiah, Mishael, and Azariah, his companions:

Dan. 2:18   That they would desire mercies of the God of heaven concerning this secret; that Daniel and his fellows should not perish with the rest of the wise men of Babylon.

At once, the king agreed to give Daniel a little more time to meditate on the situation. Daniel went to his friends and explained the situation to them. They did not want to perish with the other wise men, so they prayed to God, seeking the contents of the king's dream and its interpretation. Their quick action parallels with Proverbs 3:5–6, which states, "Trust in the LORD with all thine heart; and lean not unto thine own understanding. In all thy ways acknowledge him, and he shall direct thy paths."

Dan. 2:19	Then was the secret revealed unto Daniel in a night vision. Then Daniel blessed the God of heaven.
Dan. 2:20	Daniel answered and said, Blessed be the name of God for ever and ever: for wisdom and might are his:
Dan. 2:21	And he changeth the times and the seasons: he removeth kings, and setteth up kings: he giveth wisdom unto the wise, and knowledge to them that know understanding:
Dan. 2:22	He revealeth the deep and secret things: he knoweth what is in the darkness, and the light dwelleth with him.
Dan. 2:23	I thank thee, and praise thee, O thou God of my fathers, who hast given me wisdom and might, and hast made known unto me now what we desired of thee: for thou hast now made known unto us the king's matter.

Without delay, God revealed the dream and its interpretation to Daniel in a night vision. Daniel gave praise and thanksgiving to God for answering his prayer in such a timely manner. He blessed the name of the Lord who lives forever and ever. He acknowledged that the God of Abraham, Isaac, and Jacob, is full of all wisdom and might. Nothing is impossible to him. He can change times and seasons. He can establish kings and remove kings at his desire. Only he can reveal secret things, and only he can shine the light on things that's engulfed in darkness. He is LORD of all.

Dan. 2:24	Therefore Daniel went in unto Arioch, whom the king had ordained to destroy the wise men of Babylon: he

went and said thus unto him; Destroy not the wise men of Babylon: bring me in before the king, and I will shew unto the king the interpretation.

Dan. 2:25   Then Arioch brought in Daniel before the king in haste, and said thus unto him, I have found a man of the captives of Judah, that will make known unto the king the interpretation.

Daniel approached Arioch and requested that he delay the execution of the wise men. He also asked permission to see the king at once so that he could reveal to the king, his dream and its interpretation. Arioch hurried Daniel in to see the king. He informed the king that he had discovered one of the captives of Judah who could divulge the contents of the king's dream and disclose the interpretation of it.

Dan. 2:26   The king answered and said to Daniel, whose name was Belteshazzar, Art thou able to make known unto me the dream which I have seen, and the interpretation thereof?

Dan. 2:27   Daniel answered in the presence of the king, and said, The secret which the king hath demanded cannot the wise men, the astrologers, the magicians, the soothsayers, shew unto the king;

Dan. 2:28   But there is a God in heaven that revealeth secrets, and maketh known to the king Nebuchadnezzar what shall be in the latter days. Thy dream, and the visions of thy head upon thy bed, are these;

Dan. 2:29   As for thee, O king, thy thoughts came into thy mind upon thy bed, what should come to pass hereafter: and he that revealeth secrets maketh known to thee what shall come to pass.

Dan. 2:30   But as for me, this secret is not revealed to me for any wisdom that I have more than any living, but for their sakes that shall make known the interpretation to the

king, and that thou mightest know the thoughts of thy
heart.

The king motioned to Daniel as if to say, if you're not capable of
revealing the dream and its interpretation then don't waste my time. Daniel
informed the king that he knew his wise men could not disclose the dream's
contents, but there is a God in heaven that reveal secrets. The purpose of
the king's vision was that God is showing to the king, things that would
happen in the days to come. The substance of the king's dream were things
that were prophetic in nature. Daniel also assured the king that he's no
wiser than anyone else, but God used him to reveal the king's dream and
its interpretation.

The Dream's Contents

Dan. 2:31   Thou, O king, sawest, and behold a great image. This
            great image, whose brightness was excellent, stood
            before thee; and the form thereof was terrible.
Dan. 2:32   This image's head was of fine gold, his breast and his
            arms of silver, his belly and his thighs of brass,
Dan. 2:33   His legs of iron, his feet part of iron and part of clay.
Dan. 2:34   Thou sawest till that a stone was cut out without hands,
            which smote the image upon his feet that were of iron
            and clay, and brake them to pieces.
Dan. 2:35   Then was the iron, the clay, the brass, the silver, and
            the gold, broken to pieces together, and became like
            the chaff of the summer threshingfloors; and the wind
            carried them away, that no place was found for them:
            and the stone that smote the image became a great
            mountain, and filled the whole earth.

Daniel revealed the contents of the forgotten dream to King
Nebuchadnezzar. In his dream, the king saw a great image. The image had

a beautiful appearance and it stood before the Lord. The mere presence of the image sparked fear in all who witnessed it. Daniel continued by describing the image. The head of the statute consisted of fine gold. His breast and his arms were of silver. His belly and his thighs were of brass. His legs were of iron, and his feet were of part iron and part clay.

The image that the king saw in his dream remained in authority for an extended period. It remained in place until a stone that was cut out without human hands confronted the image by attacking its feet. The entire structure consisted of gold, silver, brass, iron, and clay, but its feet were of iron and clay, the weakest part of the structure. The stone broke the feet of the image into many pieces, resulting in the entire image crumbling to the ground. The destruction of the image reduced it into many very tiny pieces so that it became like the chaff of the threshing floors, and the wind blew the dust away. No trace of the image existed anymore. The stone that struck the image on its feet became a high mountain and filled the whole earth.

The Dream's Interpretation

Dan. 2:36   This is the dream; and we will tell the interpretation thereof before the king.

Dan. 2:37   Thou, O king, art a king of kings: for the God of heaven hath given thee a kingdom, power, and strength, and glory.

Dan. 2:38   And wheresoever the children of men dwell, the beasts of the field and the fowls of the heaven hath he given into thine hand, and hath made thee ruler over them all. Thou art this head of gold.

Daniel proceeds with the interpretation of the dream. King Nebuchadnezzar was a king of kings. The God of heaven had given him a kingdom that was full of power, strength, and glory. It was the God of heaven who made Nebuchadnezzar ruler over the entire territory. He was in authority over everything found in this kingdom; including all the people, all the beasts, and all the fowls of the air. Nebuchadnezzar was the leader or head over the entire territory; therefore, he was the head of gold of this great image.

Dan. 2:39   And after thee shall arise another kingdom inferior to thee, and another third kingdom of brass, which shall bear rule over all the earth.

Dan. 2:40   And the fourth kingdom shall be strong as iron: forasmuch as iron breaketh in pieces and subdueth all things: and as iron that breaketh all these, shall it break in pieces and bruise.

At that present time, King Nebuchadnezzar was the head of gold, who was reigning over the entire territory. Another kingdom would succeed Nebuchadnezzar's kingdom. The arms and breast of the great image of silver referenced the new empire. The second kingdom would be inferior to the head of gold. After the second kingdom, there would be a third kingdom that was referenced by the image's belly and thighs that were made of brass. The third kingdom would also reign over all the earth for a season. After the third kingdom, there would be a fourth kingdom, referenced by the image's legs of iron. The fourth kingdom would be as strong as iron. Just as iron subdues things by breaking them into pieces, the fourth kingdom would also be forceful, but its inevitable destiny was total annihilation. The stone crafted without human intervention would break the fourth kingdom into pieces.

The extraordinary image that Nebuchadnezzar saw in his dream was symbolic for all of the world's kingdoms that would reign over Israel. It included a period from the kingdom of Babylon, up to and including the end of the world as we presently know it. Each of the respective body parts of the great image represented a different kingdom, and each of these kingdoms would exercise supremacy over the land of Israel.

Dan. 2:41   And whereas thou sawest the feet and toes, part of
             potters' clay, and part of iron, the kingdom shall be
             divided; but there shall be in it of the strength of the iron,
             forasmuch as thou sawest the iron mixed with miry clay.

Dan. 2:42   And as the toes of the feet were part of iron, and part
             of clay, so the kingdom shall be partly strong, and partly
             broken.

Dan. 2:43   And whereas thou sawest iron mixed with miry clay, they
             shall mingle themselves with the seed of men: but they
             shall not cleave one to another, even as iron is not mixed
             with clay.

The fourth kingdom would be strong like iron, and it would also be as weak as clay. It would be divided because iron and clay do not mix. The joining together of the seed of the iron and miry clay is a reference to arranged marriages to gain political strength. The kingdom would be partly strong and partly broken because it was unequally yoked. These arranged marriages would lead to the kingdom's ultimate downfall and annihilation. The iron mixing with the miry clay is a reference to the historical relationships between the Syrian (Seleucid) and the Egyptian (Ptolemy) kingdoms.

Dan. 2:44   And in the days of these kings shall the God of heaven
             set up a kingdom, which shall never be destroyed: and
             the kingdom shall not be left to other people, but it shall
             break in pieces and consume all these kingdoms, and it
             shall stand for ever.

Dan. 2:45   Forasmuch as thou sawest that the stone was cut out of
             the mountain without hands, and that it brake in pieces
             the iron, the brass, the clay, the silver, and the gold; the
             great God hath made known to the king what shall come
             to pass hereafter: and the dream is certain, and the inter-
             pretation thereof sure.

In the days of the fourth kingdom, the God of heaven would establish a realm that would exist forever. Humankind would not control any parts of the new dominion because it would pulverize and consume all of man's previous ideologies. Righteousness would fill this new kingdom, and it would stand forever. It is the millennial kingdom.

King Nebuchadnezzar saw in his dream a stone that was created by the hand of the Lord to destroy the image. This supernatural act was proof that God had revealed this dream to Nebuchadnezzar. This dream was prophetic and had end-time ties that are associated with the annihilation of all worldly kingdoms. The vision is genuine, and the interpretation is inevitable.

> Dan. 2:46   Then the king Nebuchadnezzar fell upon his face, and worshipped Daniel, and commanded that they should offer an oblation and sweet odours unto him.
>
> Dan. 2:47   The king answered unto Daniel, and said, Of a truth it is, that your God is a God of gods, and a Lord of kings, and a revealer of secrets, seeing thou couldest reveal this secret.

After Daniel disclosed the dream and interpretation of King Nebuchadnezzar, the king fell upon his face and worshipped Daniel. He commanded that the people present an offering and burn incense in Daniel's honor. King Nebuchadnezzar then acknowledged Daniel's God as the supreme God, because only the God that Daniel followed could reveal the secrets of humanity.

> Dan. 2:48   Then the king made Daniel a great man, and gave him many great gifts, and made him ruler over the whole province of Babylon, and chief of the governors over all the wise men of Babylon.
>
> Dan. 2:49   Then Daniel requested of the king, and he set Shadrach, Meshach, and Abednego, over the affairs of the province of Babylon: but Daniel sat in the gate of the king.

Then King Nebuchadnezzar promoted Daniel. He gave him many great gifts, and he made him ruler over the whole province of Babylon. He elevated him to chief of the governors and positioned him over all the wise men of Babylon.

CHAPTER 3

THE KING'S IMAGE

Dan. 3:1	Nebuchadnezzar the king made an image of gold, whose height was threescore cubits, and the breadth thereof six cubits: he set it up in the plain of Dura, in the province of Babylon.
Dan. 3:2	Then Nebuchadnezzar the king sent to gather together the princes, the governors, and the captains, the judges, the treasurers, the counsellers, the sheriffs, and all the rulers of the provinces, to come to the dedication of the image which Nebuchadnezzar the king had set up.
Dan. 3:3	Then the princes, the governors, and captains, the judges, the treasurers, the counsellers, the sheriffs, and all the rulers of the provinces, were gathered together unto the dedication of the image that Nebuchadnezzar the king had set up; and they stood before the image that Nebuchadnezzar had set up.

King Nebuchadnezzar's Great Image

KING Nebuchadnezzar erected an immense statue that was similar to the image he saw in his dream (Dan. 2:31–35). Only the head of the image in the king's vision was of gold, but the entire body of the statute constructed by the king was of gold. They positioned the structure in the Plain of Dura, the town's circle or town's square of the kingdom of Babylon. The height of the image was sixty cubits, and the breadth was six cubits wide. One cubit is approximately eighteen inches; therefore the image stood ninety feet tall and nine feet wide.

The image was probably an image in the likeness of the king himself because he was the head of gold (Dan. 2:38). The king's image was made exclusively of gold, and for that reason, there was a lavish dedication ceremony for the great statute. The king required that all of the governmental officials attend the dedication service. The list of officials that participated in the dedication was quite distinguished. It included princes, governors, captains, judges, treasurers, counselors, sheriffs, and all the rulers of the provinces.

A New Decree

Dan. 3:4   Then an herald cried aloud, To you it is commanded, O
            people, nations, and languages,

Dan. 3:5   That at what time ye hear the sound of the cornet,
            flute, harp, sackbut, psaltery, dulcimer, and all kinds of
            musick, ye fall down and worship the golden image that
            Nebuchadnezzar the king hath set up:

Dan. 3:6   And whoso falleth not down and worshippeth shall
            the same hour be cast into the midst of a burning fiery
            furnace.

Dan. 3:7   Therefore at that time, when all the people heard the
            sound of the cornet, flute, harp, sackbut, psaltery, and
            all kinds of musick, all the people, the nations, and the
            languages, fell down and worshipped the golden image
            that Nebuchadnezzar the king had set up.

The king's heart's desire was for everyone to bow down and worship him; therefore, he issued a new decree. He ordered messengers to go in the towns and villages and announce to all the people in several languages that when they heard the sound of a conglomeration of musical instruments, they were to bow down and worship the golden image. The burning fiery furnace awaited anyone that did not fall and worship the image. Failure to comply would result in immediate punishment, without a trial or hearing. They would face extermination in the fiery furnace without delay.

After the messengers completed their mission of broadcasting the new decree, there would be no excuses for not worshipping the golden image. Whenever the people heard the musical instruments, they were legally obligated to bow down and worship the golden image that was erected by King Nebuchadnezzar, without hesitation.

The Accusation

Dan. 3:8   Wherefore at that time certain Chaldeans came near, and accused the Jews.

Dan. 3:9   They spake and said to the king Nebuchadnezzar, O king, live for ever.

Dan. 3:10   Thou, O king, hast made a decree, that every man that shall hear the sound of the cornet, flute, harp, sackbut, psaltery, and dulcimer, and all kinds of musick, shall fall down and worship the golden image:

Dan. 3:11   And whoso falleth not down and worshippeth, that he should be cast into the midst of a burning fiery furnace.

Dan. 3:12   There are certain Jews whom thou hast set over the affairs of the province of Babylon, Shadrach, Meshach, and Abednego; these men, O king, have not regarded thee: they serve not thy gods, nor worship the golden image which thou hast set up.

When the musical instruments began to sound, everyone stopped whatever he or she were doing and bowed down to worship the golden image, except for three Hebrew captives. Shadrach, Meshach, and Abednego refused to bow down and worship the golden image. Worshipping any image was against their beliefs, so they refused to do it (Exo. 20:4–5). Scripture reveals no explanation as to why Daniel did not appear with Shadrach, Meshach, and Abednego. Perhaps he was alone, and no one witnessed him refusing to bow down and worship the image.

Some of the Chaldeans were jealous of Shadrach, Meshach, and Abednego and they wanted revenge. Shadrach, Meshach, and Abednego were foreign captives who had been promoted ahead of native Babylonian citizens (Dan. 2:49). To get revenge, the Chaldeans approached the king and reminded him of his new decree. Then they proceeded to identify Shadrach, Meshach, and Abednego as violators of the king's new law. They pointed out to the king that Shadrach, Meshach, and Abednego refused to obey the king's new ordinance because they lacked respect for the king and his gods. They willfully refused to bow down and worship the king's image, and they did it in public for all to see. Then they reminded the king of the punishment for failure to obey his new law. The Chaldean's revenge was to have Shadrach, Meshach, and Abednego destroyed in the fiery furnace.

King Nebuchadnezzar's Rage

Dan. 3:13   Then Nebuchadnezzar in his rage and fury commanded to bring Shadrach, Meshach, and Abednego. Then they brought these men before the king.

Dan. 3:14   Nebuchadnezzar spake and said unto them, Is it true, O Shadrach, Meshach, and Abednego, do not ye serve my gods, nor worship the golden image which I have set up?

Dan. 3:15   Now if ye be ready that at what time ye hear the sound of the cornet, flute, harp, sackbut, psaltery, and dulcimer, and all kinds of musick, ye fall down and worship the image which I have made; well: but if ye worship not, ye shall be cast the same hour into the midst of a burning fiery furnace; and who is that God that shall deliver you out of my hands?

King Nebuchadnezzar was furious. He commanded that Shadrach, Meshach, and Abednego present themselves before him without delay. The king presided over court proceedings to exercise due process to anyone that defied his new law. The officials prepared the charges, and the king read the charges against Shadrach, Meshach, and Abednego. They were charged with refusal to serve the Babylonian gods and refusal to worship his golden image. The king knew these men were beneficial to his kingdom, so he gave them a second chance to redeem themselves. He gave them an ultimatum. He would order the musical instruments to begin to sound again, and they were to bow down and worship the golden image. If they complied, the matter would be forgotten. Failure to do so would result in them being catapulted into the fiery furnace. To add insult to injury, the king was so adamant that they bow down and worship his image that he questioned their loyalty to their god. He was so defiant that he stated that their god could not save them from any punishment he imposed upon them.

A Plea of Fidelity

Dan. 3:16   Shadrach, Meshach, and Abednego, answered and said to the king, O Nebuchadnezzar, we are not careful to answer thee in this matter.

Dan. 3:17   If it be so, our God whom we serve is able to deliver us from the burning fiery furnace, and he will deliver us out of thine hand, O king.

Dan. 3:18   But if not, be it known unto thee, O king, that we will not serve thy gods, nor worship the golden image which thou hast set up.

Shadrach, Meshach, and Abednego responded to the king's ultimatum, but they did not address him as king. They called the king by his name. They respectfully informed the king that under no circumstances would they bow down and worship his golden image. If the king's new law commanded throwing violators in the fiery furnace, then so be it. The God that they serve could deliver them out of the fiery furnace, and he could even deliver them from under the king's authority. They concluded their statement in a more forceful tone. They stated to the king that whether their God saved them or not, they would not serve or worship the Babylonian gods or the king's golden image.

The King's Acrimony

Dan. 3:19   Then was Nebuchadnezzar full of fury, and the form
             of his visage was changed against Shadrach, Meshach,
             and Abednego: therefore he spake, and commanded that
             they should heat the furnace one seven times more than
             it was wont to be heated.

Dan. 3:20   And he commanded the most mighty men that were in
             his army to bind Shadrach, Meshach, and Abednego, and
             to cast them into the burning fiery furnace.

Dan. 3:21   Then these men were bound in their coats, their hosen,
             and their hats, and their other garments, and were cast
             into the midst of the burning fiery furnace.

Dan. 3:22   Therefore because the king's commandment was urgent,
             and the furnace exceeding hot, the flame of the fire
             slew those men that took up Shadrach, Meshach, and
             Abednego.

Dan. 3:23   And these three men, Shadrach, Meshach, and
             Abednego, fell down bound into the midst of the
             burning fiery furnace.

The king was furious, after hearing Shadrach, Meshach, and Abednego rejecting him in public court. His countenance changed against them, and he commanded that they increase the heat of the furnace until it was seven times hotter. He then ordered his most decorated soldiers to bind them with all of their clothing and catapult them into the fiery furnace.

King Nebuchadnezzar's soldiers obeyed the king's order. They tossed Shadrach, Meshach, and Abednego into the fiery furnace. The king did suffer some collateral damage with the execution of his commands. The soldiers assigned to carry out the king's orders lost their lives because the furnace was so hot that the flames engulfed them as they delivered Shadrach, Meshach, and Abednego into the fiery furnace.

The King's Amazement

Dan. 3:24   Then Nebuchadnezzar the king was astonied, and rose up in haste, and spake, and said unto his counsellers, Did not we cast three men bound into the midst of the fire? They answered and said unto the king, True, O king.

Dan. 3:25   He answered and said, Lo, I see four men loose, walking in the midst of the fire, and they have no hurt; and the form of the fourth is like the Son of God.

Immediately after the ejection of Shadrach, Meshach, and Abednego into the fiery furnace, King Nebuchadnezzar looked into the flames, and he was astonished. The king recalls throwing three bound men into the fiery furnace, but now he sees a fourth man in the raging flames. The fourth man appears to be the son of God. The king also observed that the restraints of the three men had been removed. It became apparent to the king and his subordinates that the flames had no power over Shadrach, Meshach, and Abednego. Perhaps the fourth person in the fiery furnace was the same God that King Nebuchadnezzar insisted could not save Shadrach, Meshach, and Abednego from the fiery furnace (Dan. 3:15).

A Change of Heart

Dan. 3:26   Then Nebuchadnezzar came near to the mouth of the burning fiery furnace, and spake, and said, Shadrach, Meshach, and Abednego, ye servants of the most high God, come forth, and come hither. Then Shadrach, Meshach, and Abednego, came forth of the midst of the fire.

Dan. 3:27   And the princes, governors, and captains, and the king's
            counsellers, being gathered together, saw these men,
            upon whose bodies the fire had no power, nor was
            an hair of their head singed, neither were their coats
            changed, nor the smell of fire had passed on them.

The king was traumatized by what he saw in the furnace. With caution, he approached the mouth of the burning fiery furnace. He addressed Shadrach, Meshach, and Abednego as the servants of the Most High God. He ordered them to come out of the fiery furnace and stand before him again. Then Shadrach, Meshach, and Abednego exited the fiery furnace under their own power.

The Babylonians, princes, governors, captains, and counselors witnessed this entire event. The somewhat normal execution of three men turned into a formidable admission that the flames of the fiery furnace had no power over Shadrach, Meshach, and Abednego. Their bodies suffered no burns. Their hair were not singed. Their coats sustained no damage from the raging flames. They did not have a hint of the smell of smoke on them, but the raging fire consumed the soldiers that tossed them into the furnace.

Another Decree

Dan. 3:28   Then Nebuchadnezzar spake, and said, Blessed be the
            God of Shadrach, Meshach, and Abednego, who hath
            sent his angel, and delivered his servants that trusted in
            him, and have changed the king's word, and yielded their
            bodies, that they might not serve nor worship any god,
            except their own God.

Dan. 3:29   Therefore I make a decree, That every people, nation,
            and language, which speak any thing amiss against the
            God of Shadrach, Meshach, and Abednego, shall be
            cut in pieces, and their houses shall be made a dunghill:

because there is no other God that can deliver after this sort.

Dan. 3:30   Then the king promoted Shadrach, Meshach, and Abednego, in the province of Babylon.

King Nebuchadnezzar had a new revelation. He blessed the God of Shadrach, Meshach, and Abednego. He acknowledged that it was their god who sends his angel to deliver all who place their trust in him. It was their god who reversed the king's orders and rescued them unharmed from the fiery furnace. It was their god who delivered them from the burning flames. They escaped sudden death because they refused to worship any other god, except Almighty God.

The king makes another decree (law). He declared that if anyone from any nation, speak in any language, anything amiss against the God of Shadrach, Meshach, and Abednego, they would suffer severe consequences. They would cut their bodies into pieces, and their houses would become dunghills because there is no other God who can deliver like the god of Shadrach, Meshach, and Abednego. Note, the Chaldeans' plan of revenge backfired on them. The king promoted Shadrach, Meshach, and Abednego to even higher positions in his kingdom.

CHAPTER 4

NEBUCHADNEZZAR'S DILEMMA

Dan. 4:1   Nebuchadnezzar the king, unto all people, nations, and languages, that dwell in all the earth; Peace be multiplied unto you.

Dan. 4:2   I thought it good to shew the signs and wonders that the high God hath wrought toward me.

Dan. 4:3   How great are his signs! and how mighty are his wonders! his kingdom is an everlasting kingdom, and his dominion is from generation to generation.

The Speech

KING Nebuchadnezzar was speaking to all people who lived within the borders of his kingdom and outside of the authority of his empire. He was talking to people of all nations and all languages because he wanted everyone to enjoy the same peace that he was experiencing.

He was speaking about the God of Shadrach, Meshach, and Abednego. He praised their God, and he reminded the people of the signs and wonders that God had shown him. He acknowledged that God's dominion is from generation to generation. He also recognized the fact that God's kingdom is an everlasting kingdom. Nebuchadnezzar thought it was a good idea to show the people signs and wonders about his ordeal. He spent seven years of his life living like an animal before his sanity returned to him. He wanted to share his experience with others so that they would repent from their sins.

Technically speaking, the first three verses of chapter four of the book of Daniel should be at the end rather than the beginning. Rearranging the order in this chapter broadens the message that is being conveyed. Daniel 4:4–33 shares the king's extraordinary experiences for a period of seven years because of his great pride. Daniel 4:34–37 reveals the praise the king had for the Lord after his sobering experience of total and complete humbling. Daniel 4:1–3 discloses the king's newfound love for the Lord, and the king wanted to share his experience with others with the express purpose of challenging them to repent.

The King's Nightmare

Dan. 4:4   I Nebuchadnezzar was at rest in mine house, and flourishing in my palace:

Dan. 4:5   I saw a dream which made me afraid, and the thoughts upon my bed and the visions of my head troubled me.

Dan. 4:6   Therefore made I a decree to bring in all the wise men of Babylon before me, that they might make known unto me the interpretation of the dream.

Dan. 4:7   Then came in the magicians, the astrologers, the Chaldeans, and the soothsayers: and I told the dream before them; but they did not make known unto me the interpretation thereof.

King Nebuchadnezzar had a second dream. His first dream was in chapter 2. In his vision, his kingdom was flourishing, but something caught his attention and frightened him. He was so disturbed that he awakened. Upon awakening from this nightmare, he summoned all of his wise men, magicians, astrologers, Chaldeans, and soothsayers to his bedside. He wanted an immediate interpretation of his dream. Unlike the other nightmare he experienced in chapter 2, this time the king remembered it, and all he wanted was its interpretation. Unfortunately, the wise men were not successful at interpreting the king's dream.

The Wise Men's Dilemma

Dan. 4:8   But at the last Daniel came in before me, whose name
            was Belteshazzar, according to the name of my god, and
            in whom is the spirit of the holy gods: and before him I
            told the dream, saying,

Dan. 4:9   O Belteshazzar, master of the magicians, because I know
            that the spirit of the holy gods is in thee, and no secret
            troubleth thee, tell me the visions of my dream that I
            have seen, and the interpretation thereof.

After all of the other self-proclaimed wise men failed to interpret the
king's dream, Daniel was invited to appear before the king. The Babylonian
establishment changed Daniel's name to Belteshazzar, which is the name
of King Nebuchadnezzar's god. Daniel was promoted to master of all the
wise men (Dan. 2:48). It seems odd that King Nebuchadnezzar summoned
the wise men before consulting with Daniel. He was not a magician, but
he had the powers of Almighty God working in his life. The king acknowledges that Daniel had the spirit of the "holy gods"; therefore, he requested
that Daniel interpret his dream for him.

The King's Dream

Dan. 4:10   Thus were the visions of mine head in my bed; I saw,
            and behold a tree in the midst of the earth, and the
            height thereof was great.

Dan. 4:11   The tree grew, and was strong, and the height thereof
            reached unto heaven, and the sight thereof to the end of
            all the earth:

Dan. 4:12   The leaves thereof were fair, and the fruit thereof much,
            and in it was meat for all: the beasts of the field had
            shadow under it, and the fowls of the heaven dwelt in
            the boughs thereof, and all flesh was fed of it.

Dan. 4:13   I saw in the visions of my head upon my bed, and, behold, a watcher and an holy one came down from heaven;

Dan. 4:14   He cried aloud, and said thus, Hew down the tree, and cut off his branches, shake off his leaves, and scatter his fruit: let the beasts get away from under it, and the fowls from his branches:

Dan. 4:15   Nevertheless leave the stump of his roots in the earth, even with a band of iron and brass, in the tender grass of the field; and let it be wet with the dew of heaven, and let his portion be with the beasts in the grass of the earth:

Dan. 4:16   Let his heart be changed from man's, and let a beast's heart be given unto him; and let seven times pass over him.

Dan. 4:17   This matter is by the decree of the watchers, and the demand by the word of the holy ones: to the intent that the living may know that the most High ruleth in the kingdom of men, and giveth it to whomsoever he will, and setteth up over it the basest of men.

The king begins to share the contents of his dream with Daniel. In the vision, there was a tree in the middle of the earth. The tree was exceedingly tall, and it continued to grow until the treetops reached into heaven. The tree's branches stretched forth everywhere on Planet Earth. The leaves of the tree were beautiful, and the fruit provided food for man and beast alike. All of the animals found protection from the elements by taking advantage of the tree's covering. The birds of the air discovered a safe haven amongst the tree branches where they built their nests.

Before the dream ended, Daniel witnessed an apparition within his dream. The apparition demanded the destruction of the tree by chopping it down and removing all of its branches. He also commanded that the leaves be shaken off the branches and the fruit thereof be plucked off of the branches and scattered. The animals and fowls were to be allowed to escape from under the tree before it is chopped down. The stump of the tree should remain for the preservation of its roots and metal bands were to encompass the stump of the tree. The stump must be left with the animals so that the dew will accumulate on it daily. Perhaps this is what frightened the king; the stump bound with the bands was to eat grass as if it was an animal and the stump had the heart of a man that changed to the heart of a beast. Without warning, the text switches from a decaying stump to a stump having the qualities of a human.

The apparition decreed these words in the dream because it was a command from the Holy One. This command was a sign to humanity, so there would be no doubt; it is the Most High God that rules in the kingdoms of men. God establishes realms, and over those domains, he places his authority upon whosoever he chooses; rich or poor; free or bond.

The Interpretation

Dan. 4:18   This dream I king Nebuchadnezzar have seen. Now thou, O Belteshazzar, declare the interpretation thereof, forasmuch as all the wise men of my kingdom are not able to make known unto me the interpretation: but thou art able; for the spirit of the holy gods is in thee.

The king just revealed the contents of his dream to Daniel. Now he has petitioned Daniel for its interpretation. He mentioned to Daniel that his native Babylonian wise men were not able to interpret the dream for him. The king knew Daniel was capable of understanding it because the spirit of the "holy gods" dwells within him, and Daniel had revealed the contents of his dreams and its interpretations in times past.

Dan. 4:19   Then Daniel, whose name was Belteshazzar, was astonied for one hour, and his thoughts troubled him. The king spake, and said, Belteshazzar, let not the dream, or the interpretation thereof, trouble thee. Belteshazzar

answered and said, My lord, the dream be to them
that hate thee, and the interpretation thereof to thine
enemies.

Daniel considered the dream for about an hour. He was perplexed
about the interpretation of the vision. His thoughts troubled him because
the results were not favorable to the king. It also appears the king already
knew the explanation was unfavorable. Nevertheless, the king reminded
Daniel not to try to be sentimental on his behalf when he discloses the
interpretation of the dream.

Daniel began to divulge the dream's interpretation. The vision was
about the king's enemies. Just as the king anticipated, the explanation was
against him but favorable for his enemies.

Dan. 4:20   The tree that thou sawest, which grew, and was strong,
             whose height reached unto the heaven, and the sight
             thereof to all the earth;
Dan. 4:21   Whose leaves were fair, and the fruit thereof much, and
             in it was meat for all; under which the beasts of the field
             dwelt, and upon whose branches the fowls of the heaven
             had their habitation:
Dan. 4:22   It is thou, O king, that art grown and become strong: for
             thy greatness is grown, and reacheth unto heaven, and
             thy dominion to the end of the earth.

Daniel proceeded to unveil the interpretation of the dream concerning
the tree that he saw in the middle of the earth. The tree that the king saw,
that grew strong until it reached into heaven was King Nebuchadnezzar
himself. He was the dictator of the Babylonian kingdom at that time. All
the inhabitants of the world recognized his dominion as a domineering
factor in the lives of humanity. His jurisdiction provided food and shelter
for all forms of life here on Earth. The kingdom of Babylon had grown in
greatness, and its mere presence had become a formidable force. Because

of its internal and external prominence, it had also transformed itself into a diabolical nation. Such evil had the proclivity of capturing the attention of heaven, and it did.

The tree is symbolic for a kingdom; just as the image in King Nebuchadnezzar's first dream was symbolic for all earthly domains that are controlled by man. Everything that lived in the Babylonian kingdom was under the rule of King Nebuchadnezzar. Because he managed every aspect of the people's lives, he began to think that he was a god. He was so arrogant that he forgot the fact that he was not the creator of the earth. He often felt that it was by his might and own design that he was king of Babylon. In one form or another, the Babylonian kingdom affected the lives of everyone on earth, and King Nebuchadnezzar was their king.

Dan. 4:23　　And whereas the king saw a watcher and an holy one coming down from heaven, and saying, Hew the tree down, and destroy it; yet leave the stump of the roots thereof in the earth, even with a band of iron and brass, in the tender grass of the field; and let it be wet with the dew of heaven, and let his portion be with the beasts of the field, till seven times pass over him;

Dan. 4:24　　This is the interpretation, O king, and this is the decree of the most High, which is come upon my lord the king:

Dan. 4:25　　That they shall drive thee from men, and thy dwelling shall be with the beasts of the field, and they shall make thee to eat grass as oxen, and they shall wet thee with the dew of heaven, and seven times shall pass over thee, till thou know that the most High ruleth in the kingdom of men, and giveth it to whomsoever he will.

The watcher is an angel, and the Holy One is God. The angel came down from heaven to declare judgment upon the kingdom. The decree came from the Most High God. The order was to hew the tree down and destroy it but to leave the stump and the roots in the earth. Then, bands of iron and brass were to be fastened around the stump of the tree. The stump that remained after the tree's removal was wet with the dew of heaven, and the king's provision was with the beasts of the field. The stump was to remain powerless until seven times passed over him.

The interpretation is two-fold. It talked of a tree that's cut down, leaving only a stump. The stump is the remains of the Babylonian kingdom. King Nebuchadnezzar was the king of Babylon, but he would lose his sanity and would be driven from the presence of man because he began to mimic the behavior of a wild animal. He lived outdoors where dew accumulated on his back every night. His portion of food was the grass of the field, and he would dine with the other animals. He would live outdoors with the animals until seven times (years) transpired. That's how long it would take for him to understand that it is an unequivocal fact that the Almighty God rules in the kingdoms of men in any capacity that he so chooses. He would also realize that Almighty God can create or destroy anybody or anything at his discretion.

The tree is symbolic for all world kingdoms under the control of man. This tree was also known as the Babylonian kingdom. The tree (Babylon) would be cut down or overthrown. Multiple scriptures prophesy the fall of Babylon (Isa. 21:9; Jer. 5:8; Rev. 14:8; 18:2).

The tree is also symbolic for King Nebuchadnezzar. He was the leader of the Babylonian kingdom. He would lose his authority for a period of seven years. The kingdom would still exist, but Nebuchadnezzar would not control it because he would experience some mental challenges.

Dan. 4:26   And whereas they commanded to leave the stump of the tree roots; thy kingdom shall be sure unto thee, after that thou shalt have known that the heavens do rule.

Dan. 4:27   Wherefore, O king, let my counsel be acceptable unto thee, and break off thy sins by righteousness, and thine iniquities by shewing mercy to the poor; if it may be a lengthening of thy tranquillity.

The tree is the kingdom of Babylon. Leaving the stump in the earth symbolizes that the kingdom has lost its authority, but life still remains in it. The stump is what would remain of the Babylonian empire after it fell. The stump that was left with the bands around it confirmed that the kingdom still wasn't completely dead. It would take King Nebuchadnezzar seven years before he acknowledged that God was sovereign, and after that, his sanity would return to him. Note, these events concerning the Babylonian kingdom mirrors the seven years of tribulation that will take place during the end times. That will be a time when man will experience strong delusion (2Th. 2:11).

After the restoration of King Nebuchadnezzar's sanity, he proclaimed some soul-saving advice to the people of the world. He begged them to listen to him because he was speaking from experience. His advice to the people was for them to repent from their sins and iniquities and begin living a lifestyle of righteousness by showing mercy and kindness to the poor. It was repentance that would bring lasting tranquility and prosperity on the earth.

The Manifestation of the Dream

Dan. 4:28   All this came upon the king Nebuchadnezzar.

Dan. 4:29   At the end of twelve months he walked in the palace of the kingdom of Babylon.

Dan. 4:30   The king spake, and said, Is not this great Babylon, that I have built for the house of the kingdom by the might of my power, and for the honour of my majesty?

Dan. 4:31   While the word was in the king's mouth, there fell a voice from heaven, saying, O king Nebuchadnezzar, to thee it is spoken; The kingdom is departed from thee.

Dan. 4:32   And they shall drive thee from men, and thy dwelling shall be with the beasts of the field: they shall make thee to eat grass as oxen, and seven times shall pass over thee, until thou know that the most High ruleth in the kingdom of men, and giveth it to whomsoever he will.

Dan. 4:33   The same hour was the thing fulfilled upon
              Nebuchadnezzar: and he was driven from men, and did
              eat grass as oxen, and his body was wet with the dew of
              heaven, till his hairs were grown like eagles' feathers, and
              his nails like birds' claws.

King Nebuchadnezzar's dream manifested itself, just as Nebuchadnezzar dreamed it. The manifestation of his vision began one year after he had his nightmare. As he walked in his palace of the kingdom of Babylon, he started to become exceedingly prideful. He credited himself with building the kingdom of Babylon with his own power and abilities. While the words were in the king's mouth, he heard a voice from heaven, stating he lost control of his kingdom. He would be driven from living among people, and he would live with the beasts of the field, eating grass as an ox. Seven years would pass before he would acknowledge that Almighty God is the only one who rules in the kingdoms of men. It is the Lord that gives dominions to whomsoever he will.

The same hour that the voice from heaven spoke to King Nebuchadnezzar, the dream began to manifest itself upon the king. He lost his sanity, and they drove him from the comfortable living quarters of his palace. He ate grass with the oxen. The dew accumulated on his body every night. His hairs began to grow like eagle's feathers, and his fingernails and toenails started to become like the claws of a bird. The preservation of the kingdom was guaranteed, but King Nebuchadnezzar was no longer in control of it.

A Change of Heart

Dan. 4:34   And at the end of the days I Nebuchadnezzar lifted up mine eyes unto heaven, and mine understanding returned unto me, and I blessed the most High, and I praised and honoured him that liveth for ever, whose dominion is an everlasting dominion, and his kingdom is from generation to generation:

Dan. 4:35   And all the inhabitants of the earth are reputed as
             nothing: and he doeth according to his will in the army
             of heaven, and among the inhabitants of the earth: and
             none can stay his hand, or say unto him, What doest
             thou?

Dan. 4:36   At the same time my reason returned unto me; and for
             the glory of my kingdom, mine honour and brightness
             returned unto me; and my counsellers and my lords
             sought unto me; and I was established in my kingdom,
             and excellent majesty was added unto me.

Dan. 4:37   Now I Nebuchadnezzar praise and extol and honour
             the King of heaven, all whose works are truth, and his
             ways judgment: and those that walk in pride he is able to
             abase.

At the end of seven years, King Nebuchadnezzar lifted his eyes unto heaven. After the restoration of his sanity, he began to bless the Most High God. He decided that he would praise and honor Almighty God because it is he who lives forever. Nebuchadnezzar also acknowledged that God's dominion is an everlasting dominion. God's kingdom would reign from generation to generation, and his reign is not limited to one term. His authority is continuous, and it spans throughout all ages.

God is supreme. The powers and abilities of humanity are considered to be nothing when compared to the power and authority of Almighty God. He does according to his will, with his heavenly army in heaven and with the inhabitants of the earth. No one can stay the hand of God or question him as to what he's doing or why he's doing it.

King Nebuchadnezzar continued to praise, worship, and thank God for being merciful to him. When his sanity returned unto him, his counselors and lords restored him in the palace again. From that point forward, the king had a renewed sense of honor and dignity for Almighty God. Nebuchadnezzar praised, extolled, and honored the King of heaven because he knows that all of the Lord's works are truth, and all of his ways are judgment. God can debase anyone who walks in pride, and there are no exceptions.

The fourth chapter of the book of Daniel should have concluded with verses one through three, where King Nebuchadnezzar was telling the story to his countrymen. It should have begun with verses 4–37 because it speaks of the dream and events that followed. In verses 1–3, Nebuchadnezzar explains his change of heart after God dealt explicitly with him to expose his *pride*.

Summary of Chapter 4

In Daniel 4:1–3, the king explained the sovereignty of God. In Daniel 4:4–9, the king had a nightmare, and he began seeking the interpretation of the dream. Daniel 4:10–18 reveals the contents of the king's dream. Daniel 4:19–27 discloses the understanding of the vision. Daniel 4:28–33 provides the manifestation of his nightmare, and Daniel 4:34–37 displays the king's appreciation for the Most High God.

The tree in the middle of the earth is the kingdom of Babylon. The tree is symbolic for all worldly kingdoms on earth. The cutting down of the tree is to make room for a second kingdom. The stump of the tree is to signify that the Babylonian kingdom is no longer the kingdom in power, but its roots are still alive. The bands of brass and iron on the stump represent the third and fourth kingdoms, respectively. King Nebuchadnezzar's dream in this chapter parallels with his previous vision of the great image (Dan. 2:31–45). The destruction of the kingdom of Babylon never ends until the return of Christ.

As recorded in chapter 2, Babylon is the head of Gold, the first earthly kingdom to have domineering control over the nation of Israel. Babylon is also the last earthly kingdom that would exercise total control over the land of Israel. It will be manifested again as the Antichrist's kingdom. Just as the first Babylonian kingdom fell, the last one will also disintegrate as recorded in Revelation 14:8 and Revelation 18:2. King Nebuchadnezzar's dream in chapter 2 is synonymous with his vision in chapter 4. See Appendix F for the parallels of Nebuchadnezzar's dreams.

CHAPTER 5

THE HANDWRITING ON THE WALL

Dan. 5:1	Belshazzar the king made a great feast to a thousand of his lords, and drank wine before the thousand.
Dan. 5:2	Belshazzar, whiles he tasted the wine, commanded to bring the golden and silver vessels which his father Nebuchadnezzar had taken out of the temple which was in Jerusalem; that the king, and his princes, his wives, and his concubines, might drink therein.
Dan. 5:3	Then they brought the golden vessels that were taken out of the temple of the house of God which was at Jerusalem; and the king, and his princes, his wives, and his concubines, drank in them.
Dan. 5:4	They drank wine, and praised the gods of gold, and of silver, of brass, of iron, of wood, and of stone.

The Banquet

BELSHAZZAR organized a massive party for the members of his cabinet. Please do not confuse Belshazzar with Belteshazzar. Belshazzar was the king of Babylon. Belteshazzar is Daniel. There is something else to note; the book of Daniel is not written in chronological order. The following verses confirm the non-chronological order of the book of Daniel.

Dan. 7:1   records the *first year* of Belshazzar, king of Babylon

Dan. 8:1   records the *third year* of the reign of King Belshazzar

Dan. 5:30   recorded the *death* of King Belshazzar

The order of events listed above, actually affirms that Daniel chapters 7 and 8 occurred before Daniel chapter 5. Belshazzar's reign ended the night of his great party, the same night he died (Dan. 5:30). See Appendix A for the possible chronological order of the chapters in the book of Daniel.

The following scriptures seem to indicate that Belshazzar was King Nebuchadnezzar's son, rather than his grandson.

Dan. 5:2   which *his father* Nebuchadnezzar had taken

Dan. 5:11   whom King Nebuchadnezzar; *thy father*

Dan. 5:18   God gave Nebuchadnezzar *thy father*

Dan. 5:21   and thou *his son, O Belshazzar*

History reveals to us that Belshazzar was the grandson of King Nebuchadnezzar. His father' name was Nabonidus, and he was Nebuchadnezzar's oldest son. Belshazzar and Nabonidus were co-rulers of the kingdom of Babylon. Nabonidus reigned as king of Babylon from 555–539 BC.[9]

Let's take a closer look at the words *son* and *father*. In Greek, the word *son* #G5207 means "kinship or a descendant." Matthew 1:1 states, "The book of the generation of Jesus Christ, the son of David, the son of Abraham." Jesus was not the immediate son of David or Abraham, but he was a descendant of David and Abraham." Belshazzar was a descendant of King Nebuchadnezzar, not necessarily his son but his grandson.

In Greek, the word *father* #G3962 means "a parent." A parent can be either near or remote. Jesus referenced the scribes and Pharisees as being in the likeness of their father, the devil. Surely Jesus was not insinuating their

---

[9] *Nelson's New Illustrated Bible Dictionary* (Thomas Nelson Publisher, 1986), 170, 171.

biological father was the devil, but he was alluding to their mimicking the teachings and deeds of the devil, which was their father figure.

Jeremiah, 27:7 states, "And all nations shall serve him, and his son, and his son's son, until the very time of his land come: and then many nations and great kings shall serve themselves of him." This verse shows a direct correlation of the reign over the kingdom of Babylon by Nebuchadnezzar's son and grandson. King Nebuchadnezzar was the father, Nabonidus was his son, and Belteshazzar was his grandson.

The text continues with Belshazzar, King of Babylon, honoring a thousand of his opulent and influential businessmen, his princes, his wives, and his concubines with an extravagant party. He exceeded expectation by providing excessive amounts of everything for his distinguished guests. He ordered his servants to use the gold and silver vessels for his guests to consume their alcoholic beverages. These gold and silver vessels were the holy vessels that were confiscated by King Nebuchadnezzar during the Babylonian invasion of Jerusalem (Dan. 1:1–2).

The intended purpose of these vessels was to be used only in God's temple. Their purpose was not to be used by foreigners to consume wine at a social gathering. As they drank their wine from the holy vessels, they began to praise the gods of gold, the gods of silver, the gods of brass, the gods of iron, the gods of wood, and the gods of stone. There was no mention of Almighty God, although they were consuming alcoholic beverages out of his holy vessels.

The Handwriting on the Wall

Dan. 5:5   In the same hour came forth fingers of a man's hand, and wrote over against the candlestick upon the plaister of the wall of the king's palace: and the king saw the part of the hand that wrote.

Dan. 5:6   Then the king's countenance was changed, and his thoughts troubled him, so that the joints of his loins were loosed, and his knees smote one against another.

Dan. 5:7   The king cried aloud to bring in the astrologers, the
            Chaldeans, and the soothsayers. And the king spake,
            and said to the wise men of Babylon, Whosoever
            shall read this writing, and shew me the interpretation
            thereof, shall be clothed with scarlet, and have a chain
            of gold about his neck, and shall be the third ruler in the
            kingdom.

Dan. 5:8   Then came in all the king's wise men: but they could not
            read the writing, nor make known to the king the inter-
            pretation thereof.

Dan. 5:9   Then was king Belshazzar greatly troubled, and his coun-
            tenance was changed in him, and his lords were astonied.

At the same hour when Belshazzar's guests began to drink wine from
the holy vessels and praised false gods, there appeared a hand out of thin
air, and it began to write on the wall of the palace. All of a sudden, the
king's countenance changed because this unexplained phenomenon frightened him. He was so afraid that his knees began to tremble to the point
that they were knocking against each other. To make matters worse, the
king lost control of his bowels in front of all of his distinguished guests.

The king managed to gain control of his faculties, and he commanded
that all the wise men, including the astrologers, Chaldeans, and soothsayers
appear before him at once. As they entered and stood before the king, he
proposed a covenant with them. A handsome reward awaited anyone who
could read the writing on the wall and provide its interpretation. The victorious person would be clothed with scarlet and would be given a chain of
gold to wear around his neck. He would also be promoted to be the third
ruler in the kingdom of Babylon.

The wise men studied and pondered the writing on the wall, but they
were unable to read it, much less interpret it. The wise men's inability to
reveal the writing to the king troubled him even more. It was apparent that
the mysterious writing on the wall had a significant meaning, but its interpretation evaded the king and his guests, causing them to be overwhelmed.

Dan. 5:10   Now the queen, by reason of the words of the king
            and his lords, came into the banquet house: and the
            queen spake and said, O king, live for ever: let not
            thy thoughts trouble thee, nor let thy countenance be
            changed:

Dan. 5:11   There is a man in thy kingdom, in whom is the spirit of
            the holy gods; and in the days of thy father light and
            understanding and wisdom, like the wisdom of the gods,
            was found in him; whom the king Nebuchadnezzar thy
            father, the king, I say, thy father, made master of the
            magicians, astrologers, Chaldeans, and soothsayers;

Dan. 5:12   Forasmuch as an excellent spirit, and knowledge, and
            understanding, interpreting of dreams, and shewing
            of hard sentences, and dissolving of doubts, were
            found in the same Daniel, whom the king named
            Belteshazzar: now let Daniel be called, and he will shew
            the interpretation.

Belshazzar sent for the queen. She was probably the king's mother
or perhaps his grandmother. As the queen entered the palace, Belshazzar
explained the situation to her. Perhaps he forgot to mention that they
were drinking wine from the holy vessels. He began to explain to her that
a mysterious hand appeared from nowhere and wrote some unknown
writing on the wall of the palace. He explained that he summoned the wise
men to read it and interpret it for to him, but they were perplexed by the
writing also.

The countenance of the king's guests, revealed to the queen just how
much the handwriting had frightened them. Perhaps she even smelled what
a profound effect it had directly upon the king himself. She also understood
that the wise men's inability to read and interpret the writing made matters
even worse. As soon as the queen recognized the gravity of the situation, she embraced Belshazzar to console him in front of his guests. She
instructed the king that he should not be troubled by the fact that the wise

men could not interpret the handwriting. She proceeded to tell him that there is a man in his kingdom, who possesses the spirit of the holy gods. This man whose name is Daniel possesses the light and understanding of Almighty God. He previously revealed to King Nebuchadnezzar a dream that he had forgotten, and then he proceeded to give the interpretation of the dream. The king recognized that Daniel possessed the spirit of knowledge and understanding. He was so overwhelmed with Daniel that he promoted him to be master over all of his wise men.

She informed the king that Daniel had already proven himself by interpreting dreams and solving riddles. He has revealed the contents and interpretation of even the toughest mysteries. She impressed upon Belshazzar that if he summoned Daniel to come to the banquet floor; he would show him the meaning and interpretation of the handwriting on the wall.

Daniel Appears before King Belshazzar

Dan. 5:13   Then was Daniel brought in before the king. *And* the king spake and said unto Daniel, *Art* thou that Daniel, which *art* of the children of the captivity of Judah, whom the king my father brought out of Jewry?

Dan. 5:14   I have even heard of thee, that the spirit of the gods *is* in thee, and *that* light and understanding and excellent wisdom is found in thee.

Dan. 5:15   And now the wise *men*, the astrologers, have been brought in before me, that they should read this writing, and make known unto me the interpretation thereof: but they could not shew the interpretation of the thing:

Dan. 5:16   And I have heard of thee, that thou canst make interpretations, and dissolve doubts: now if thou canst read the writing, and make known to me the interpretation thereof, thou shalt be clothed with scarlet, and *have* a chain of gold about thy neck, and shalt be the third ruler in the kingdom.

Daniel was summoned to stand before Belshazzar. The king insisted that Daniel verified that he was not an imposter. Belshazzar asked Daniel whether or not he was one of the captives King Nebuchadnezzar brought from Judah. Then he mentioned that he had heard of his exploits and he knew that the spirits of the gods dwell within him. The king proceeded to offer Daniel a substantial reward if he could read the handwriting on the wall and reveal the interpretation of the writing. The prospective reward consisted of Daniel's promotion to the third ruler in the kingdom of Babylon, and he would be clothed in scarlet attire with a gold chain to wear around his neck. Belshazzar offered Daniel the same deal that he offered his other not-so-wise men.

The king explained the situation to Daniel. While the king and his guests were socializing, there appeared some mysterious writing on the wall. They did not understand the appearance of the writing or the meaning of it. He summoned his wise men, but they could not read it, let alone interpret it. The writing was of a different nature because no one in the banquet hall could read it. Belshazzar was so distraught that he forgot to mention to Daniel that they were drinking wine from the holy vessels, when the mysterious hand appeared and wrote the writing on the wall.

The History of the Kingdom

Dan. 5:17   Then Daniel answered and said before the king, Let thy gifts be to thyself, and give thy rewards to another; yet I will read the writing unto the king, and make known to him the interpretation.

Dan. 5:18   O thou king, the most high God gave Nebuchadnezzar thy father a kingdom, and majesty, and glory, and honour:

Dan. 5:19   And for the majesty that he gave him, all people, nations, and languages, trembled and feared before him: whom he would he slew; and whom he would he kept alive; and whom he would he set up; and whom he would he put down.

Dan. 5:20   But when his heart was lifted up, and his mind hardened
              in pride, he was deposed from his kingly throne, and
              they took his glory from him:

Dan. 5:21   And he was driven from the sons of men; and his heart
              was made like the beasts, and his dwelling was with the
              wild asses: they fed him with grass like oxen, and his
              body was wet with the dew of heaven; till he knew that
              the most high God ruled in the kingdom of men, and
              that he appointeth over it whomsoever he will.

Daniel informed the king that he did not want any compensation for his services. He assured the king that he would read the writing on the wall and reveal to him the interpretation, but he did not want the king's gifts. He insisted that the king redistribute his rewards to someone else.

Daniel then proceeded to give Belshazzar a lesson in history and humility by reminding him of the ordeals that his grandfather experienced. Almighty God blessed Nebuchadnezzar (Belshazzar's grandfather) with a kingdom, filled with majesty, dignity, and honor. Under King Nebuchadnezzar's rule, all people, nations, and languages trembled and feared him. He alone decided who lived and who died in his kingdom. He promoted and endorsed whomever he chose. He exercised his authority and dominion over all business and social transactions under the jurisdiction of his kingdom. Nevertheless, Nebuchadnezzar's continued praising himself to the point that his heart was hardened with pride.

The king experienced deposition from his kingly throne and his glory removed from him (Dan. 4:28–33). Daily activities challenged his mind, and he began to act as though he was inhuman. His insanity progressed to the point that palace officials drove him from living in the royal palace. His fate was to dwell outside with the animals. He resided and dined with the donkeys and oxen. Because he lived outside with the animals, every morning his body would be covered with the dew from heaven. These things continued until Nebuchadnezzar recognized and acknowledged that all power and authority belongs to the Most High God. He succumbed to the fact that it is the Lord who establishes all kingdoms. It is Almighty God who appoints whomsoever he will to be the leader of any kingdom that he establishes.

King Nebuchadnezzar was in this unusual state of mind for seven years. When he realized that Almighty God was sovereign, his sanity returned to him. He then acknowledged that he was just a pawn in the chessboard of life. He understood that it is God who establishes kingdoms and allows individuals to rise to become kings. God did not have to allow Nebuchadnezzar to become king of Babylon. He could have chosen someone else to be king of Babylon if he so desired.

Dan. 5:22 And thou his son, O Belshazzar, hast not humbled thine heart, though thou knewest all this;

Dan. 5:23 But hast lifted up thyself against the Lord of heaven; and they have brought the vessels of his house before thee, and thou, and thy lords, thy wives, and thy concubines, have drunk wine in them; and thou hast praised the gods of silver, and gold, of brass, iron, wood, and stone, which see not, nor hear, nor know: and the God in whose hand thy breath is, and whose are all thy ways, hast thou not glorified:

Dan. 5:24 Then was the part of the hand sent from him; and this writing was written.

Belshazzar was King Nebuchadnezzar's grandson. Armed with the facts of what happened to his grandfather, he should have been a little more humble, but he too hardened his heart against the things of the Lord. Although he knew that King Nebuchadnezzar's pride cause him to experience a mental breakdown and expulsion from his kingdom, that did not deter Belshazzar from lifting himself against the Lord of heaven. At his request, Belshazzar's servants brought the holy vessels confiscated from God's house into the banquet hall. Then the king, his lords, his wives, and his concubines proceeded to drink alcoholic beverages from those vessels as they praised other gods.

Belshazzar followed in his grandfather's footsteps because he praised the gods of silver, gold, brass, iron, wood, and stone, instead of praising Almighty God. The Babylonian gods that he praised could not see, hear, or comprehend anything because they are objects shaped and formed by the imagination and hands of man. Belshazzar did not glorify Almighty God, even though his next breath depended upon him. It is the Lord who gives everyone the ability to do everything, but Belshazzar rejected the Lord outright. For that reason, the Lord sent the hand to write on the wall.

The Interpretation

Dan. 5:25   And this is the writing that was written, MENE, MENE, TEKEL, UPHARSIN.

Dan. 5:26   This is the interpretation of the thing: MENE; God hath numbered thy kingdom, and finished it.

Dan. 5:27   TEKEL; Thou art weighed in the balances, and art found wanting.

Dan. 5:28   PERES; Thy kingdom is divided, and given to the Medes and Persians.

Daniel begins to read the message on the wall so that he can give Belshazzar the interpretation. The contents of the writing on the wall are:

MENE MENE TEKEL UPHARSIN

After Daniel read the writing on the wall, he then proceeded to give Belshazzar the interpretation of the writing.

- MENE   #H4484   numbered
- TEKEL   #H8625   balances
- UPHARSIN   #H6537   to split up; to divide

When Daniel gives the interpretation, he substituted *Peres* with the word *Upharsin*. Peres and Upharsin have the same meaning—both have the same Strong's number #H6537. The singular form of the word is *Peres*. The plural form of the word is *Upharsin*.

The interpretation of the handwriting on the wall is as follows:

MENE: God hath numbered your kingdom; and finished it.

In the original writing, mene appears twice. Perhaps the first mene means the kingdom is numbered and the second mene means the kingdom is finished. In the interpretation, Daniel only used the word *mene* once, but it has a double meaning. It means the kingdom is numbered, and the kingdom is fallen. Perhaps mene mene indicates that the days of two individuals have come to an end; Nebuchadnezzar and Belshazzar himself.

TEKEL: thou art weighed in the balances, and art found wanting.

Being weighed in the balances is a direct reference to Belshazzar. He was in debt to God because he did not accept him as Lord and Savior. Now the kingdom was about to be stripped from him. His debt was due, and a pardon was out of the question. Full payment was due immediately; even if he had to pay with his life (Dan. 5:30.)

PERES: thy kingdom is divided and given to the Medes and Persians.

The kingdom of Babylon will cease to exist. The Medes and the Persians will overthrow the kingdom of Babylon. The succession of the Medes and Persians is a historical fact, and it also affirms that Almighty God can—and will—give any kingdom to whomsoever he desires.

The Regime Change

Dan. 5:29   Then commanded Belshazzar, and they clothed Daniel with scarlet, and put a chain of gold about his neck, and made a proclamation concerning him, that he should be the third ruler in the kingdom.

Dan. 5:30   In that night was Belshazzar the king of the Chaldeans slain.

Dan. 5:31   And Darius the Median took the kingdom, being about threescore and two years old.

After Daniel read the handwriting on the wall and gave Belshazzar its interpretation, the king fulfilled his promise to Daniel, concerning his reward for interpreting the handwriting. Without any pomp and circumstance, Daniel received a promotion to the third ruler in the Babylonian kingdom. They clothed him in scarlet attire and placed a gold chain around his neck. Daniel had previously stated that he did not want any compensation. Perhaps he did not complain because he knew the overthrow of the Babylonian kingdom was imminent. It happened that very night. That same night, Belshazzar the king of the Chaldeans was slain and Darius the Median took the Babylonian kingdom. The takeover by Darius was the affirmation that Daniel's interpretation of the handwriting on the wall was correct. Darius was about sixty-two years old when he overthrew the Babylonian Kingdom.

Now, there was a balance of power in the region. Babylon was no longer the supreme power. The Babylonian kingdom was divided, and the succeeding kingdom consisted of two nations: the Medes and Persians. The name of the new kingdom was the Medo-Persian kingdom.

Please note, Daniel did receive his promotion to the third ruler in the Babylonian kingdom, but it was short-lived. The overthrow of the Babylonian kingdom occurred that very night. Perhaps it did not matter to Daniel because he had already stated that he did not want any gifts or rewards from Belshazzar for interpreting the handwriting on the wall.

CHAPTER 6

THE LION'S DEN

Dan. 6:1   It pleased Darius to set over the kingdom an hundred
            and twenty princes, which should be over the whole
            kingdom;
Dan. 6:2   And over these three presidents; of whom Daniel was
            first: that the princes might give accounts unto them,
            and the king should have no damage.
Dan. 6:3   Then this Daniel was preferred above the presidents and
            princes, because an excellent spirit was in him; and the
            king thought to set him over the whole realm.

A New Cabinet

DARIUS the Mede, has just completed the overthrow of the
Babylonian kingdom (Dan. 5:30–31). He was now king of a newly
established kingdom, known as the Medo-Persian kingdom. His cabinet
consisted of a hundred and twenty princes to reign over his entire kingdom,
and they answered to three presidents. The three presidents would give
account to the king so that the king would have no problems. Of those
three presidents, Daniel was first in command. He was preferred above
the other presidents and princes because he possessed an excellent spirit.
It is important to note, Belshazzar of the Babylonian Kingdom promoted
Daniel to be third in rank, but overnight he was promoted to be second in
rank, and he was a Hebrew foreigner.

King Darius' Watergate

Dan. 6:4   Then the presidents and princes sought to find occa-
            sion against Daniel concerning the kingdom; but they
            could find none occasion nor fault; forasmuch as he was
            faithful, neither was there any error or fault found in
            him.

Dan. 6:5   Then said these men, We shall not find any occa-
            sion against this Daniel, except we find it against him
            concerning the law of his God.

Two of the presidents and the hundred and twenty princes sought
to bring an accusation against Daniel. They were jealous of him because
he was a former foreign slave, and now he became their superior. As they
sought ways to discredit him, it became apparent that Daniel was faithful
to the king. Daniel was so scrupulous in his honesty that their attempt to
bring accusations against him were short-circuited. Because Daniel was so
loyal to the king, they had to conjure another way to discredit him. They
decided to use Daniel's strengths against him. Daniel was faithful to the
king, but he was even more so faithful to his God. For that reason, his
subordinates hatched a diabolical plan, where they would manufacture a
situation, forcing Daniel's loyalty to the king to conflict with his loyalty to
his god.

Dan. 6:6   Then these presidents and princes assembled together to
            the king, and said thus unto him, King Darius, live for ever.

Dan. 6:7   All the presidents of the kingdom, the governors, and
            the princes, the counsellers, and the captains, have
            consulted together to establish a royal statute, and to
            make a firm decree, that whosoever shall ask a petition
            of any God or man for thirty days, save of thee, O king,
            he shall be cast into the den of lions.

Dan. 6:8   Now, O king, establish the decree, and sign the writing,

that it be not changed, according to the law of the
Medes and Persians, which altereth not.

Dan. 6:9   Wherefore king Darius signed the writing and the
decree.

Dan. 6:10   Now when Daniel knew that the writing was signed, he
went into his house; and his windows being open in his
chamber toward Jerusalem, he kneeled upon his knees
three times a day, and prayed, and gave thanks before his
God, as he did aforetime.

Two of the presidents and the hundred and twenty princes assembled
to conjure their nefarious plan against Daniel. They decided to make a new
law concerning religious worship within the Medo-Persian kingdom. They
crafted the new law in such a way that it would force Daniel to either be
loyal to the laws of the kingdom or be loyal to the laws of his God.

They appeared before Darius with their diabolical plan. They explained
to the king that all of the leaders agreed to enact a new law; a law that
would establish King Darius as sovereign. Please note, they did not inform
the king that Daniel did not have a hand in crafting the new law. They
made it sound as though Daniel was in agreement. The new law would
forcibly confine anyone in the lion's den, who asked a petition or prayed
to any god or man, except King Darius, within a thirty-day period. They
requested that King Darius establish the new decree and sign it into law as
soon as possible. Under the already-established laws of the Medo-Persian
kingdom, a nullification of a new law is impossible, even if the new law was
injurious to the kingdom.

This evil gang of leaders did not hold to the same standards of loyalty
as Daniel. According to the law of the Medes and Persians, this whole
meeting violated the chain of command. The hundred and twenty princes
were to report to the three presidents, and the three presidents are to
agree before any new legislation reach the king. Daniel had no role in the
new legislation, and Daniel was not at the meeting with King Darius. The
unsavory leaders insisted that King Darius sign the new decree into law.

The king did succumb to their request, and he signed the decree into law, thinking his entire cabinet had scrutinized it, just as any other new legislation, before being presented to the king.

It is evident that Daniel was not present at the signing of the new law because he would have objected to it. After ratification of the new law, Daniel went into his house and opened his window in the chamber toward Jerusalem. First Kings 8:44 states, "If thy people go out to battle against their enemy, whithersoever thou shalt send them, and shall pray unto the LORD toward the city which thou hast chosen, and toward the house that I have built for thy name." Daniel prayed toward the house of God that was located at Jerusalem. It was habitual for him to pray to his god three times daily. This day was no different. He kneeled upon his knees and gave thanks to his God, just as he did every day before the ratification of the new law. Daniel knew he violated the laws of the kingdom that he swore to uphold, but this was a diabolical law. It was conceived by deceitful means to make him choose between loyalty to the kingdom or to his God. He chose to be loyal to his God, even though the penalty was capital punishment.

Dan. 6:11   Then these men assembled, and found Daniel praying and making supplication before his God.

Dan. 6:12   Then they came near, and spake before the king concerning the king's decree; Hast thou not signed a decree, that every man that shall ask a petition of any God or man within thirty days, save of thee, O king, shall be cast into the den of lions? The king answered and said, The thing is true, according to the law of the Medes and Persians, which altereth not.

This gang of conspirators strategically assembled themselves and found Daniel praying and making supplication before his God. They proceeded to call an emergency meeting to accuse Daniel of violating the king's new law. They began their accusation by reminding the king of the new law. They asked the king, "Hast thou not signed a decree, that every man that shall ask a petition of any God or man within thirty days, save of thee, O king, shall be cast into the den of lions?" Notice, they even included the consequences for violating the new law.

The king informed them that they were correct. He did sign a new decree into law. Then they countered by reminding him that according to the law of the Medes and Persians, upon enactment of new legislation, it cannot be changed. Perhaps the king thought they wanted to amend the law for some unknown reason because he reminded them that alteration of the law is impossible. Furthermore, the law was only temporary; it would expire in thirty days. As a general rule, temporary laws are usually crafted to fulfill a specific agenda. In this instance, it was drafted to entrap Daniel for the sole purpose of circumventing his authority—forever.

Dan. 6:13   Then answered they and said before the king, That Daniel, which is of the children of the captivity of Judah, regardeth not thee, O king, nor the decree that thou hast signed, but maketh his petition three times a day.

Dan. 6:14   Then the king, when he heard these words, was sore displeased with himself, and set his heart on Daniel to deliver him: and he laboured till the going down of the sun to deliver him.

Dan. 6:15   Then these men assembled unto the king, and said unto the king, Know, O king, that the law of the Medes and Persians is, That no decree nor statute which the king establisheth may be changed.

When the king informed the conspirators that the law was immutable, they then proceeded to accuse Daniel of acting in a way that was unbecoming for a governmental official. They drafted up several new charges against him. First, they reminded the king that Daniel was not a native Medo-Persian. He is one of the captives from the children of Judah. Second, they informed the king that Daniel served a different God than the Medes and Persians. Third, they informed the king that Daniel did not regard the king or the kingdom's laws. Fourth, they informed the king that Daniel violated the new law by petitioning his God instead of petitioning the king as determined by the new decree. They informed the king that Daniel was in defiance of the new law because he continued to pray to his God three times a day, even after the implementation of the new law.

King Darius was hesitant to have Daniel arrested. He sought ways of exonerating Daniel from the consequences of the new decree. Daniel's conspirators continued by pressing the king that according to the laws of the Medes and Persians, no law or statute could be modified. They pointed out that Daniel has proceeded to violate the king's new law and he was still not under arrest. King Darius found himself to be in a state of acrimony for signing the new decree into law.

> Dan. 6:16   Then the king commanded, and they brought Daniel, and cast him into the den of lions. Now the king spake and said unto Daniel, Thy God whom thou servest continually, he will deliver thee.
>
> Dan. 6:17   And a stone was brought, and laid upon the mouth of the den; and the king sealed it with his own signet, and with the signet of his lords; that the purpose might not be changed concerning Daniel.

After the conspirators insisted that Daniel not be treated as though he was above the law, the king commanded the arrest of Daniel without delay. Daniel was apprehended and brought before the king. Darius held a formal hearing, and it was determined that Daniel did, in fact, violate the new law, and he must suffer the consequences. The king pronounced Daniel's sentence. He was to be remanded to the lion's den. Then the king broke protocol. He asked Daniel whether or not the god to whom he dedicated his loyalty was capable of delivering him from the den of ferocious lions. The king proceeded to order the guards to escort Daniel to the lion's den. After Daniel's confinement in the lion's den and the gate was secured, a massive stone was rolled in place to cover the mouth of the den. The king's seal and the seal of the princes were stamped upon the stone to prevent an internal procedural error from causing Daniel to be prematurely released.

Dan. 6:18   Then the king went to his palace, and passed the night fasting: neither were instruments of musick brought before him: and his sleep went from him.

Dan. 6:19   Then the king arose very early in the morning, and went in haste unto the den of lions.

Dan. 6:20   And when he came to the den, he cried with a lamentable voice unto Daniel: *and* the king spake and said to Daniel, O Daniel, servant of the living God, is thy God, whom thou servest continually, able to deliver thee from the lions?

Dan. 6:21   Then said Daniel unto the king, O king, live for ever.

Dan. 6:22   My God hath sent his angel, and hath shut the lions' mouths, that they have not hurt me: forasmuch as before him innocency was found in me; and also before thee, O king, have I done no hurt.

Dan. 6:23   Then was the king exceeding glad for him, and commanded that they should take Daniel up out of the den. So Daniel was taken up out of the den, and no manner of hurt was found upon him, because he believed in his God.

Dan. 6:24   And the king commanded, and they brought those men which had accused Daniel, and they cast *them* into the den of lions, them, their children, and their wives; and the lions had the mastery of them, and brake all their bones in pieces or ever they came at the bottom of the den.

After Daniel's confinement in the lion's den, the king went to his palace. Perhaps he experienced what could be classified as the longest night of his life because he could not sleep. He rejected the soft music that was played for him daily, and he passed the time reminiscing and fasting. The next morning the king arose very early in the morning and went in haste to the den of lions. Not being able to see Daniel, the king called out his name with an unsure voice. He acknowledged Daniel as a servant of the living God whom he served without ceasing. He did not see Daniel, but he screamed to the top of his voice, asking if his God was able to deliver him from the hungry lions.

Daniel gave the king some much-needed relief when he paid homage to the king. He proceeded to tell the king that his god had shut the mouths of the lions, and he had suffered no injuries from them. Daniel continued by informing the king that his only crime was honoring the Lord with his prayers, and his intentions were not to be disrespectful to the king. Darius was exceeding glad that Daniel was not injured, and he ordered his release from the lion's den at once. The king acknowledged that Daniel's protection from the lions was because of one reason only; he trusted in his God.

The wheels of justice sometimes appear to work at the pace of an injured snail. At the king's command, his servants summoned the conspirators to his chambers. He presided over a brief hearing and determined the conspirators to be diabolical men. He then proceeded to pronounce a harsh sentence on them for their nefarious deeds. All of those men, along with their wives and children, were to receive the same fate they wished upon Daniel. All of them were awarded reservations in the lion's den. The lions enjoyed a smorgasbord—buffet style. They devoured their prey as fast as they were tossed into their den. Bear in mind; the lions had not eaten all night; they had a huge appetite, and they ate to their fill.

There is something else to note, the fate of the mischievous conspirators received the death penalty per Old Testament scripture. Any false witness must suffer the same penalty assigned to their victims (Deu. 19:16–20.)

A New Decree

Dan. 6:25   Then king Darius wrote unto all people, nations, and languages, that dwell in all the earth; Peace be multiplied unto you.

Dan. 6:26   I make a decree, That in every dominion of my kingdom men tremble and fear before the God of Daniel: for he is the living God, and stedfast for ever, and his kingdom that which shall not be destroyed, and his dominion shall be even unto the end.

Dan. 6:27   He delivereth and rescueth, and he worketh signs and wonders in heaven and in earth, who hath delivered Daniel from the power of the lions.

Dan. 6:28   So this Daniel prospered in the reign of Darius, and in the reign of Cyrus the Persian.

King Darius only wanted peace for all the people regardless of their country of origin or the language they spoke. He made a new decree. He established a national religion. Darius declared that in every dominion of his kingdom, men and women alike, should tremble and fear the God of Daniel. His God is the one and only God, and he lives and reigns forever. His kingdom cannot suffer destruction. He delivers, and he rescues. He orchestrates signs and wonders in heaven and on earth. It was Almighty God, the one and only God that delivered Daniel from the power of the lions.

Daniel continued to prosper in the reign of Darius the Mede, and he also prospered in the reign of Cyrus the Persian. Although Daniel was a foreigner and a captive from Judah, he served with dignity and honor under the jurisdiction of two different kingdoms and several dictators. Throughout the entire book of Daniel, he remained loyal to his God, and he enjoyed a multitude of blessings, awarded to him by Almighty God.

CHAPTER 7

DANIEL'S FIRST DREAM

Dan. 7:1   In the first year of Belshazzar king of Babylon Daniel
            had a dream and visions of his head upon his bed: then
            he wrote the dream, and told the sum of the matters.
Dan. 7:2   Daniel spake and said, I saw in my vision by night, and,
            behold, the four winds of the heaven strove upon the
            great sea.
Dan. 7:3   And four great beasts came up from the sea, diverse one
            from another.

THE book of Daniel consists of several dreams. It records the dreams of Nebuchadnezzar in chapters 2 and 4. Chapters 7 and 8 records Daniel's dreams. For better clarity, separate Daniel's first dream in chapter 7 into two parts. Daniel 7:1–14 gives the contents of the dream, and Daniel 7:15–28 gives the dream's interpretation.

As we study the book of Daniel, it becomes apparent that this book is not written in chronological order. Chronologically speaking, chapter 7 should precede chapter 5, because chapter 7 is about Belshazzar's first year as king of Babylon and chapter 5 is about his last night of royalty.

In the first year of Belshazzar, king of Babylon, Daniel had a dream. Belshazzar is the grandson of King Nebuchadnezzar's; therefore, this dream occurred several years after Daniel interpreted Nebuchadnezzar's dreams. This dream is the first of Daniel's two dreams as recorded in the book of Daniel.

Daniel's First Dream

In his dream, Daniel saw four winds of the heavens rush forth upon the Great Sea. The four winds are the spirit of the living God. In Hebrew, the word *Winds* mean "spirit." The Strong's reference number is #H7307. The four spirits are the four compass directions: north, south, east, and west. The four winds (spirits) are blowing upon the vast sea, which is known as the Mediterranean Sea. Confirmation of the sea's name is shown when God gives the boundaries of the nation of Israel (Num. 34:1–6). The westernmost border of Israel is the vast sea or the Mediterranean Sea.

In his dream, Daniel saw four great beasts come up from the Mediterranean Sea. It is safe to say, that the driving force for each of these four beasts is one of the four spirits, which comes from four different directions. There are four distinct beasts, and each one is unique in appearance.

Description of the Beasts

Dan. 7:4   The first was like a lion, and had eagle's wings: I beheld till the wings thereof were plucked, and it was lifted up from the earth, and made stand upon the feet as a man, and a man's heart was given to it.

The first beast had the appearance of a lion. This beast is unusual because it had wings like an eagle. Over the course of time, the beast's wings were stripped from his body. After losing his wings, he stood upon his feet as though he was a man, and began to think and act as though he was human.

Under normal circumstances, wings are a part of the body that supports flight. The meaning of the word *wings* in this verse is different. It is a symbolic reference to a season or time period when a kingdom reaches its highest level of power and authority. A better understanding of the significance of wings is that wings represent a reign or term in office. Eagles have two wings; indicating the lion had two reigns, but these two reigns are not simultaneous; they are successive.

The book of Daniel is about dreams and visions. The two dreams of King Nebuchadnezzar and the two dreams of Daniel are parallels of each other. To understand the dreams of Nebuchadnezzar is to understand the dreams of Daniel. In Daniel chapter 2, Nebuchadnezzar dreamed of a great image; it was symbolic for all the world kingdoms. Nebuchadnezzar was the leader of the first world kingdom; therefore, he was the head of gold (Dan. 2:38). Nebuchadnezzar was the leader of a great kingdom (Dan. 2:37), and the name of his kingdom was Babylon (Dan. 1:1.) There would follow a series of kingdoms after the fall of the Babylonian kingdom (Dan. 2:39–40.)

Daniel's dream in chapter 7 is identical to Nebuchadnezzar dream in chapter 2, except for the vehicles used to describe the contents of the dreams. Nebuchadnezzar's dream is about an image that represents a series of kingdoms. The different body parts of the image differentiate each kingdom, and each body part is associated with a different metal. Daniel's dream is similar to Nebuchadnezzar's dream. It, too, is about a series of kingdoms, but the difference is that in his dream, different beasts represent the kingdoms.

History tells us that Nebuchadnezzar ruled the Babylonian kingdom and after him, it was co-ruled by his son and grandson. Belshazzar was Nebuchadnezzar's grandson, and he was the primary leader of the kingdom. The wings on the back of the lion are symbolic for the two different reigns or time periods of the same kingdom. The first reign of the Babylonian kingdom was by Nebuchadnezzar, but he experienced a mental disorder. His health issues affected his cognizance, resulting in his removal from leadership, (Dan. 4:30–33.) His removal from the kingship is the plucking up of the first wing.

After Nebuchadnezzar became mentally challenged, Belshazzar ruled the Babylonian kingdom. Belshazzar died on the night that the Medo-Persian overthrew the Babylonian kingdom. When Belshazzar died, the Babylonian kingdom ceased to exist. Concerning the two wings of the beast, the first wing represents Nebuchadnezzar, and the second wing represents Belshazzar. The removal of these two wings of the beast symbolizes the end of the Babylonian kingdom. The lion is symbolic for the Babylonian kingdom, and the two wings are symbolic for the two leaders of that kingdom, Nebuchadnezzar and Belshazzar.

Daniel is having this dream in the first year of the reign of Belshazzar. The events in his dream indicate that the Babylonian kingdom remained strong and powerful after Nebuchadnezzar experienced his mental challenges, but it would eventually succumb to failure. Daniel's dream is a prophecy, foretelling the fall of the Babylonian kingdom.

> Dan. 7:5   And behold another beast, a second, like to a bear, and it raised up itself on one side, and it had three ribs in the mouth of it between the teeth of it: and they said thus unto it, Arise, devour much flesh.

The second beast had the appearance of a bear. The bear was so strong and powerful that it elevated itself by destroying everything around it. In the dream, the bear had three ribs in its mouth. The word *ribs* indicates that it is a part of a body, just as the creation of Eve came from the rib of Adam (Gen. 2:21–23). Having three ribs in its mouth indicates that the bear had conquered and devoured three other nations. From a historical viewpoint, the Medo-Persian kingdom was a combination of three nations, the Medes, the Persians, and the Babylonians. After the acquisition of the Babylonian kingdom, the Medo-Persian kingdom became the dominant power in the region.

> Dan. 7:6   After this I beheld, and lo another, like a leopard, which had upon the back of it four wings of a fowl; the beast had also four heads; and dominion was given to it.

The third beast had the appearance of a leopard. Unlike the first beast that had two wings on its back, the third beast has four wings. To make matters more grotesque, the leopard also had four heads.

The symbolism for the beast with four wings on the back has already been explained; they are four distinct time periods in the existence of a kingdom. The leopard symbolizes a kingdom, but the leopard has four heads, which symbolizes there will be four separate kingdoms. Each head along with its respective wing is the rule and reign of four separate kingdoms.

Dan. 7:7	After this I saw in the night visions, and behold a fourth beast, dreadful and terrible, and strong exceedingly; and it had great iron teeth: it devoured and brake in pieces, and stamped the residue with the feet of it: and it was diverse from all the beasts that were before it; and it had ten horns.
Dan. 7:8	I considered the horns, and, behold, there came up among them another little horn, before whom there were three of the first horns plucked up by the roots: and, behold, in this horn were eyes like the eyes of man, and a mouth speaking great things.

The fourth beast was a mighty and formidable kingdom. It was intense, aggressive and agile. It destroyed its enemies, and everything in its path became a potential sacrifice. It attacked its enemies with sophisticated weapons and tactics that reduced them to particles of dust with the dominance of his presence. The fourth beast was more vicious and calculating than the three beasts that preceded him. It overwhelmed its enemies with dominance and brutality.

Just as the three beasts that preceded the fourth beast were abnormal in appearance, the fourth beast also suffered from a deformity; it had ten horns. In the dream, Daniel witnessed another little horn beginning to sprout up in the midst of the ten horns. As the little horn grew more substantial in size, it uprooted three of the original ten horns. A beast with more than two horns is strange, but this beast is even more abnormal. The eyes of a man and a mouth that speaks with dominance are embedded in the little horn of the fourth beast.

Dan. 7:9   I beheld till the thrones were cast down, and the Ancient
            of days did sit, whose garment was white as snow, and
            the hair of his head like the pure wool: his throne was
            like the fiery flame, and his wheels as burning fire.

Dan. 7:10   A fiery stream issued and came forth from before him:
            thousand thousands ministered unto him, and ten thou-
            sand times ten thousand stood before him: the judgment
            was set, and the books were opened.

Dan. 7:11   I beheld then because of the voice of the great words
            which the horn spake: I beheld even till the beast was
            slain, and his body destroyed, and given to the burning
            flame.

Daniel observed the little horn until the destruction of his thrones
and the Ancient of Days began to reign. We know the Ancient of Days is
God because of the given description. Only Almighty God is respected,
esteemed, and hallowed at all times. His hair is white like wool, and he's
dressed in white attire. White represents righteousness (Rev. 19:8). He sits
on a fiery throne with his wheels burning. Isaiah 66:15 states, "For, behold,
the LORD will come with fire, and with his chariots like a whirlwind, to
render his anger with fury, and his rebuke with flames of fire." According to
the Hebrew, *Wheels* #1534 and #1535 is a whirlwind or something rolling.

When Christ returns, he will pour out his wrath on the little horn.
The little horn will be destroyed and confined to the burning flames. The
little horn receives this punishment because he spoke blasphemous things
against Almighty God. After the destruction of the little horn, God will
establish an everlasting kingdom, and he will reign forever. Revelation
11:15 states, "The kingdoms of this world will become the kingdoms of
Christ, and he shall reign forever and ever."

A great multitude of people who have their names recorded in the
Book of Life gathers before him. This time of fellowship parallels with
the great multitude that no man could number standing before the throne
(Rev. 7:11–12).

Dan. 7:12   As concerning the rest of the beasts, they had their
              dominion taken away: yet their lives were prolonged for
              a season and time.

Dan. 7:13   I saw in the night visions, and, behold, one like the Son
              of man came with the clouds of heaven, and came to
              the Ancient of days, and they brought him near before
              him.

Dan. 7:14   And there was given him dominion, and glory, and a
              kingdom, that all people, nations, and languages, should
              serve him: his dominion is an everlasting dominion,
              which shall not pass away, and his kingdom that which
              shall not be destroyed.

The first three beasts that Daniel witnessed coming out of the sea had
their dominion stripped away from them. Even though they suffered the
confiscation of their power and authority, a remnant of their dominion
remained intact. Their ideology still lived on, and it is still influencing
humanity.

Daniel saw something else. He saw someone that had the appearance
of the Son of Man traveling through the clouds of heaven, and this parallels with the return of Christ. Matthew 24:30 states, "And then shall appear
the sign of the Son of man in heaven: and then shall all the tribes of the
earth mourn, and they shall see the Son of man coming in the clouds of
heaven with power and great glory." The Son of Man is Jesus, the Son, and
the Ancient of Days is God, the Father. As Jesus approached the throne of
God, he will receive power, glory and an everlasting kingdom. The inhabitants of his kingdom include people from every town and village of the
entire earth, and they will serve him forever.

The Interpretation of Daniel's First Dream

Dan. 7:15   I Daniel was grieved in my spirit in the midst of my
              body, and the visions of my head troubled me.

Dan. 7:16   I came near unto one of them that stood by, and asked
              him the truth of all this. So he told me, and made me
              know the interpretation of the things.

Daniel 7:1–14 reveals the entire dream. Daniel 7:15–28 provides the interpretation of the dream. After his dream, Daniel was confused because he did not understand what the dream meant. He saw someone standing near him, so he requested the meaning of his dream or vision. Scripture does not provide the identity of this person or entity at this time. Perhaps Daniel was in the spirit or the throne room of heaven; therefore, he is referencing an angel or another heavenly being. Perhaps the heavenly being is Gabriel, one of the archangels. In Daniel's second dream or vision, a man also appeared to give Daniel the meaning of his dream. This time the man's identity was made known. His name is Gabriel (Dan. 8:15–16).

The individual Daniel saw begins to reveal the meaning of the dream to Daniel. He started by repeating the entire dream then he gave him the interpretation. Daniel's curiosity was about to get the best of him, but the individual Daniel saw satisfied that curiosity by divulging the true meaning of the dream.

Dan. 7:17   These great beasts, which are four, are four kings, which
              shall arise out of the earth.

The four beasts in Daniel's dream are four kings that will emerge from the earth. The four kings will rule over four different kingdoms. In scripture, beasts are symbolic for kingdoms, and each beast represents a different kingdom. The first beast is the first kingdom, and its mascot is a lion. The second beast is the second kingdom, and its mascot is a bear. The third beast is the third kingdom, and its mascot is a leopard. Note, the fourth beast is also a kingdom, but it has no association with an animal as its mascot.

The four kingdoms shall emerge from the Mediterranean Sea and establish their kingdoms in the region of the Middle East. The kingdom is not a literal resurrection from the sea; it is the establishment of a kingdom from the region of the Mediterranean Sea. Kingdoms are usually a confederation of nations that's unified in a common cause.

Every kingdom has a king. The four kingdoms emerge from the region of the sea, (Dan. 7:3), but the four kings emerge from the earth (Dan. 7:17). The kings of each kingdom are either a native citizen or a self-installed political leader. Such leaders are men like Osama Bin Laden and leaders of organizations like ISIS.

> Dan. 7:18   But the saints of the most High shall take the kingdom, and possess the kingdom for ever, even for ever and ever.

The saints of the Most High God will conquer the kingdom and dwell in it forever. The overthrown kingdom is the kingdom of the fourth beast. The fourth kingdom is the last kingdom on earth before Christ returns to establish his everlasting kingdom. The following verses affirm the fall of the last earthly kingdom that's ruled by man and the beginning of the Millennial Kingdom.

> Dan. 7:9   I beheld till the thrones were cast down, and the Ancient of days did sit, whose garment *was* white as snow, and the hair of his head like the pure wool: his throne *was like* the fiery flame, *and* his wheels *as* burning fire.
>
> Dan. 7:10   A fiery stream issued and came forth from before him: thousand thousands ministered unto him, and ten thousand times ten thousand stood before him: the judgment was set, and the books were opened.

> Rev. 7:9   After this I beheld, and, lo, a great multitude, which no man could number, of all nations, and kindreds, and people, and tongues, stood before the throne, and before

the Lamb, clothed with white robes, and palms in their hands;

Rev. 7:10   And cried with a loud voice, saying, Salvation to our God which sitteth upon the throne, and unto the Lamb.

Rev. 11:15   And the seventh angel sounded; and there were great voices in heaven, saying, The kingdoms of this world are become *the kingdoms* of our Lord, and of his Christ; and he shall reign for ever and ever.

After the destruction of the final earthly kingdom that's controlled by man, the millennial kingdom will be established. In that kingdom, Christ will be the king, and the saints will rule and reign with him for one thousand years (Rev. 20:4).

Dan. 7:19   Then I would know the truth of the fourth beast, which was diverse from all the others, exceeding dreadful, whose teeth were of iron, and his nails of brass; which devoured, brake in pieces, and stamped the residue with his feet;

Dan. 7:20   And of the ten horns that were in his head, and of the other which came up, and before whom three fell; even of that horn that had eyes, and a mouth that spake very great things, whose look was more stout than his fellows.

The fourth beast was more dreadful than the three beasts that preceded it. When it mounted an attack, it was ferocious and unyielding because its teeth was as strong as iron and his nails were as sharp as brass. He would rip his victim to shreds with his dictatorial authority. It would trample upon its enemies until they crumbled into very tiny pieces. Note: the iron teeth and the brass nails are associated with the belly and thighs of brass and the legs of iron of the image in Nebuchadnezzar's dream (Dan. 2:32). This description signifies that the fourth beast is a remnant of the third kingdom that preceded it.

In the beginning, the fourth beast had ten horns, but another little horn began to materialize. As the little horn grew, it uprooted three of the original ten horns. The little horn seemed to have a mind of its own because it had eyes and a mouth. It was quite domineering, and the other seven horns yielded to its every command.

| Dan. 7:21 | I beheld, and the same horn made war with the saints, and prevailed against them; |
| Dan. 7:22 | Until the Ancient of days came, and judgment was given to the saints of the most High; and the time came that the saints possessed the kingdom. |

Daniel continued to observe the little horn until it declared a successful war on the saints. The little horn is Antichrist, and the war that he waged on the saints is the Great Tribulation. The types of weaponry he deployed against the saints are military, famine, rationing, and outright genocide. Antichrist will prevail until Almighty God intervenes. When he arrives, he will pronounce judgment on the Antichrist, and the saints of the Highest will then take possession of the kingdom, and they will reign with Christ (Rev. 20:4).

Dan. 7:23	Thus he said, The fourth beast shall be the fourth kingdom upon earth, which shall be diverse from all kingdoms, and shall devour the whole earth, and shall tread it down, and break it in pieces.
Dan. 7:24	And the ten horns out of this kingdom are ten kings that shall arise: and another shall rise after them; and he shall be diverse from the first, and he shall subdue three kings.
Dan. 7:25	And he shall speak great words against the most High, and shall wear out the saints of the most High, and think to change times and laws: and they shall be given into his hand until a time and times and the dividing of time.

Dan. 7:26   But the judgment shall sit, and they shall take away his dominion, to consume and to destroy it unto the end.

Dan. 7:27   And the kingdom and dominion, and the greatness of the kingdom under the whole heaven, shall be given to the people of the saints of the most High, whose kingdom is an everlasting kingdom, and all dominions shall serve and obey him.

Dan. 7:28   Hitherto is the end of the matter. As for me Daniel, my cogitations much troubled me, and my countenance changed in me: but I kept the matter in my heart.

The man continues by explaining the identity of the fourth beast. It is the fourth and final kingdom upon earth, under the bondage of man's wisdom. Antichrist governs the final kingdom, and his kingdom is more vicious than any former kingdoms. During his reign, the world's economic and political conditions will reach an all-time low (Mat. 24:21). His reign of terror will last for a time and times and the dividing of times. *Time* is one (1) year; *time(s)* is two (2) years; *dividing of times* is one-half year. That's a total of three and one-half years that Antichrist's reign will be dominant, and it will have a negative impact on the entire world. It will tear down institutions and ideas that took centuries to build. Many people will relent to his tactics, but a few will endure until the very end.

Although the Antichrist will have the entire world in turmoil, he will not be directly reigning over the entire world. In most instances, the word *earth* means a specific land, ground, territory, region; not the entire globe. Note the phrase—*everybody in town was there*. This phrase is not inclusive of the entirety of the people. It is not referencing 100 percent of all individuals; it's referencing a large majority. Antichrist will not rule the entire globe. He will have authority over approximately 25 percent of the earth's population (Rev. 6:8). Although his authority covers only a quarter of the earth, his egregious behavior trickles down to the other seventy-five percent of the people.

The ten horns out of the fourth kingdom are ten kings that shall emerge. In Bible prophecy, the word *horns* are symbolic for kings or countries. Ten kings (countries) will rise to power, and they will form a coalition. Some examples of coalitions in the world today are NATO, SEATO, United Nations, ISIL, and so forth. These groups are composed of many different nationalities, but they are united in one common goal. The goal of this ten-nation kingdom is to destroy the nation of Israel.

Once the ten-nation coalition is formed and begins to establish its agenda, another king (little horn) shall rise after them. He will be diverse from the other leaders of the ten-nation coalition. He will subdue three kings of the ten-nation coalition and assume absolute authority over the entire coalition (kingdom). This king (little horn) is the Antichrist. He will speak great words against Almighty God (Dan. 7:8, 11, 20; Rev. 13:5–7). He will cause many people to defect from being followers of Christ (Dan. 7:21). He will change the times and laws of many religious organizations, especially the Jewish faith (Dan. 7:25). He will exalt himself by persuading the people that he is the only real god (2Th. 2:4).

When the Lord has endured enough of the Antichrist's shenanigans, he will return for his saints. He will pronounce sentence on the Antichrist and his kingdom (fourth kingdom). The Lord will commence administering his judgment upon the Antichrist and his followers by pouring out his wrath upon them. Then the Lord and the saints shall take away the dominion of Antichrist and establish an everlasting kingdom. The Antichrist's punishment is confinement in the bottomless pit for one thousand years (Rev. 20:1–3).

Even after the dream is explained to Daniel, his mental state was still a little foggy. He had a better understanding of the dream, but there was still a lot that he did not understand. It became apparent to him that his dream was about the end-times. Perhaps he was wondering whether or not the end-times were near at hand. Nevertheless, Daniel did not forget the dream or the dream's interpretation.

Summary of Chapter Seven

The four beasts represent four kingdoms (Dan. 7:17). Daniel's dream about the four beasts is associated with King Nebuchadnezzar's dream of the great image (Dan. 2:31–34). The image's head of fine gold in Nebuchadnezzar's first dream is the first kingdom. The breast and arms made of silver is the second kingdom. The belly and thighs made of brass is the third kingdom. The legs made of iron is the fourth kingdom. The feet and toes are connected to the legs of iron (Dan. 7:41–42). A little horn will emerge from the ten toes (Dan. 7:8).

A description of Nebuchadnezzar's image is given in (Dan. 2:36–40). The image represents the entirety of the world kingdoms that had a dominating effect upon Israel. God had given Nebuchadnezzar a kingdom. Because he was the head of the kingdom, he was the head of gold. Babylon is the name of the first kingdom, and that name corresponds with the first beast that looked like a lion (Dan. 7:4). The lion is symbolic for the Babylonian kingdom.

After the collapse of the Babylonian Kingdom, a second kingdom will rise to power (Dan. 2:39). The second kingdom is the breast and arms of silver (Dan. 2:32). The second kingdom corresponds to the second beast that looks like a bear (Dan. 7:5). The bear is symbolic for the Medo-Persian kingdom.

After the fall of the second kingdom, a third kingdom will rise to power (Dan. 39). The third kingdom is the belly and thighs of brass (Dan. 2:32). The third kingdom corresponds with the third beast that looks like a leopard (Dan. 7:6). The leopard is symbolic for the Grecian kingdom.

After the defeat of the third kingdom, a fourth kingdom will rise to power (Dan. 2:40). The fourth kingdom is known as the legs of iron (Dan. 2:33). The fourth kingdom corresponds with the fourth beast that was dreadful and terrible (Dan. 7:7).

Symbolism

A *beast* is a kingdom or coalition with a specific leadership or governing body. A *head* is the leader of the kingdom. A *horn* is a nation or country that is part of a kingdom. Sometimes it is used to identify the country, and sometimes it is used to identify the leadership of that country. As an example, the United States is a part of NATO. Sometimes the US president's place of business is referenced as the White House, and other times it referenced as the Oval Office. Although they are referenced by different terms, the meaning is the same. The symbolism for *wing* is a period or season of reign. An example of a wing is the Old Testament is the age of the law. The New Testament is the age of grace. A thousand years is the *millennium age*. Here is an example of the utilization of wing in scripture; the lion with two wings references the Babylonian kingdom. The first wing was King Nebuchadnezzar's reign and the second wing is his grandson Belshazzar's reign.

The bear had three ribs in its mouth (Dan. 7:5). The ribs in his mouth indicate that an enemy had been apprehended and devoured. Its defeat placed it under the power and authority of its captors; therefore the three ribs in its mouth are equivalent to the annexation of an enemy with its captor to become a part of something greater than itself. This annexation is what happened in history. The Medo-Persian kingdom was established by the annexation of three countries. The three countries that were united are Media, Persia, and Babylon. These three countries are reflective of the three ribs in the bear's mouth.

The leopard had four heads and four wings (Dan. 7:6). The four heads are four kingdoms, and the four wings are four distinct periods or times of rule. The four heads and their respective wings are congruent. The multiple heads indicate that the kingdom was unorganized with no decisive leadership. It dwarfed into four smaller kingdoms within a kingdom.

After a long period amid much chaos, the governing body of the fourth beast emerges. It is a coalition of ten horns or ten kings (Dan. 7:7). After the establishment of the fourth beast's kingdom, a clear leader of the kingdom surfaces. He is the little horn, who is a dominant leader, and he will take possession of the kingdom by uprooting three of the original ten horns (Dan. 7:8). He will establish himself as a dreadful and terrible leader. He is the Antichrist. The fourth beast is the fourth head and fourth wing of the leopard.

CHAPTER 8

DANIEL'S SECOND DREAM

Dan. 8:1	In the third year of the reign of king Belshazzar a vision appeared unto me, even unto me Daniel, after that which appeared unto me at the first.
Dan. 8:2	And I saw in a vision; and it came to pass, when I saw, that I was at Shushan in the palace, which is in the province of Elam; and I saw in a vision, and I was by the river of Ulai.

Daniel's Second Dream

IN the third year of the reign of King Belshazzar, Daniel had another dream or vision. It was quite similar to the dream he previously had in chapter 7. Daniel was a captive in Babylon. He lived in the palace at Shushan in the province of Elam. The location of the palace of Shushan is near the Ulai River.

Dan. 8:3	Then I lifted up mine eyes, and saw, and, behold, there stood before the river a ram which had two horns: and the two horns were high; but one was higher than the other, and the higher came up last.
Dan. 8:4	I saw the ram pushing westward, and northward, and southward; so that no beasts might stand before him, neither was there any that could deliver out of his hand; but he did according to his will, and became great.

Chapter 8 is Daniel's second dream. His first dream was in chapter 7. In this dream Daniel saw a ram with two horns standing near the Ulai River. There was something odd about the horns. They did not grow at the same rate or at the same time. The first horn grew to maturity, and then the second horn grew up, but it grew taller than the first horn.

It is apparent the ram was positioned in the east because it pushed toward the north, toward the south and west. The ram was robust and sturdy. He fought against his enemies and prevailed against all of them. He intimidated them all; therefore, they would not unite together to war against him. All of them surrendered to his enormous strength, making him the king of the region.

Dan. 8:5   And as I was considering, behold, an he goat came from the west on the face of the whole earth, and touched not the ground: and the goat had a notable horn between his eyes.

Dan. 8:6   And he came to the ram that had two horns, which I had seen standing before the river, and ran unto him in the fury of his power.

Dan. 8:7   And I saw him come close unto the ram, and he was moved with choler against him, and smote the ram, and brake his two horns: and there was no power in the ram to stand before him, but he cast him down to the ground, and stamped upon him: and there was none that could deliver the ram out of his hand.

Daniel saw a male goat traveling from west to the east at a very high rate of speed. It was moving so fast that it appeared not to be touching the ground. Unlike a healthy goat, this goat only had one horn, and it was quite distinguishing.

The male goat with one horn ran directly into the ram that had two horns of unequal length. He was traveling at a high rate of speed, and he approached the ram with all his fury, anger, and frustration. When he collided with the ram, the collision caused the breakage of the ram's two horns. The goat continued to trample the ram until it was lifeless.

Dan. 8:8   Therefore the he goat waxed very great: and when he was strong, the great horn was broken; and for it came up four notable ones toward the four winds of heaven.

Dan. 8:9   And out of one of them came forth a little horn, which waxed exceeding great, toward the south, and toward the east, and toward the pleasant land.

Dan. 8:10   And it waxed great, even to the host of heaven; and it cast down some of the host and of the stars to the ground, and stamped upon them.

The male goat was quite vehement, and he grew in power and strength at a very rapid pace. When the goat reached peak strength, his one notable horn was broken. With the breakage of the goat's one horn, four more prominent horns replaced it. The four new horns positioned themselves in the four compass directions: north, south, east, and west.

Out of one of the four notable horns came forth another little horn. The little horn advanced with excessive superiority and was full of pride. The little horn was skilled in advancing its agenda and convincing others to support it.

The little horn knew no boundaries; he advanced his agenda toward the south, east, and toward the nation of Israel. He did not stop there; he also expressed his contempt and disdain for the things of the Lord. He orchestrated a strategy that would cause many of the followers of God to defect from the truth.

Dan. 8:11   Yea, he magnified himself even to the prince of the
host, and by him the daily sacrifice was taken away, and
the place of his sanctuary was cast down.

Dan. 8:12   And an host was given him against the daily sacrifice by
reason of transgression, and it cast down the truth to
the ground; and it practised, and prospered.

The little horn magnified himself even to Almighty God. He was
responsible for abolishing the daily sacrifice. He harbored much disdain
for the Hebrew people and worked to destroy the sanctuary. He positioned
a group of people in place to enforce the abolishment of the daily sacrifice.
In his regime, the only truth was his doctrine as he continued to advance
in power and strength.

Dan. 8:13   Then I heard one saint speaking, and another saint said
unto that certain saint which spake, How long shall be
the vision concerning the daily sacrifice, and the transgression of desolation, to give both the sanctuary and
the host to be trodden under foot?

Dan. 8:14   And he said unto me, Unto two thousand and three
hundred days; then shall the sanctuary be cleansed.

In his dream, Daniel heard a conversation between two saints. One
saint asked a series of questions. He enquired as to how long would the
little horn continue to abandon the daily sacrifice, how long will he allow
the rebellion of destruction to continue, and how long will he trample the
sanctuary under foot? The other saint's response to the first saint is that
all of these atrocities would continue for two thousand and three hundred
days. After that, the cleansing of the sanctuary would begin.

Daniel is in a Semi-Conscious State

Dan. 8:15   And it came to pass, when I, even I Daniel, had seen the vision, and sought for the meaning, then, behold, there stood before me as the appearance of a man.

Dan. 8:16   And I heard a man's voice between the banks of Ulai, which called, and said, Gabriel, make this man to understand the vision.

Dan. 8:17   So he came near where I stood: and when he came, I was afraid, and fell upon my face: but he said unto me, Understand, O son of man: for at the time of the end shall be the vision.

Dan. 8:18   Now as he was speaking with me, I was in a deep sleep on my face toward the ground: but he touched me, and set me upright.

Dan. 8:19   And he said, Behold, I will make thee know what shall be in the last end of the indignation: for at the time appointed the end shall be.

It appears that Daniel's dream is complete, but he's not fully awake. All of a sudden, he saw a figure with the appearance of a man standing before him. He realized that he had been dreaming, but now he is seeking the dream's interpretation. Then a man's voice proceeded from the direction of the Ulai River. The voice instructed Gabriel to make Daniel understand the vision. After the man's voice spoke to Gabriel, the figure came and stood near him. Daniel was startled out of his wits and became so weak that he fell face down to the ground. Then Gabriel spoke directly to Daniel. He said, "Understand, O son of man: for at the time of the end shall be the vision."

While Gabriel was speaking to Daniel, he was in a deep sleep. Perhaps he did not hear what Gabriel said to him. Then Gabriel touched Daniel, and he regained consciousness. Once again, Gabriel spoke to Daniel saying,

"Behold, I will make thee know what shall be in the last end of the indignation: for at the time appointed the end shall be."

The Interpretation of Daniel's Second Dream

Dan. 8:20   The ram which thou sawest having two horns are the kings of Media and Persia.

Gabriel begins by explaining to Daniel that the ram with two horns is symbolic for the kings of Media and Persia (Medo-Persian kingdom). One horn represents the Medes, and the other horn represents the Persians. The nation of Persia changed its name to Iran around 1935. At the time Daniel received the vision, he was under King Belshazzar of the Babylonian kingdom. Daniel knew from King Nebuchadnezzar's dream that another kingdom will succeed the Babylonian kingdom (Dan. 2:39). The ram with two unequal horns is symbolic for the Medo-Persian kingdom. Perhaps the shorter horn is Cyrus of Persia and the taller horn is Darius of the Medes. This parallels with Darius coming to power after King Cyrus.

Dan. 8:21   And the rough goat is the king of Grecia: and the great horn that is between his eyes is the first king.

The rough goat with one horn is the king of Greece. Alexander the Great ruled the Grecian kingdom. The goat with one horn (Grecian kingdom) traveled quite swiftly from a westerly direction with the intention of making war with the ram with two horns (Medo-Persian kingdom). At the conclusion of the war, the ram's two horns were broken, which was the overthrow of the Medo-Persian kingdom, and the Grecian kingdom was born. The goat with one horn is symbolic for the Grecian kingdom.

Over the course of time, the goat's one horn was also broken. The broken horn is a reference to the death of Alexander the Great, which was the downfall of the Grecian kingdom.

Dan. 8:22   Now that being broken, whereas four stood up for it, four kingdoms shall stand up out of the nation, but not in his power.

After the death of Alexander the Great, the Grecian kingdom still existed but without a leader. With the breaking of the single horn (death of Alexander the Great), four more horns stood up and replaced it. The division of the Grecian Kingdom and its distribution to the four generals is synonymous with the growth of four horns after the breaking of the first horn. Although there are four new leaders (kingdoms), they do not have the same power as the first king (Alexander the Great).

Dan. 8:23   And in the latter time of their kingdom, when the transgressors are come to the full, a king of fierce countenance, and understanding dark sentences, shall stand up.

After the four kingdoms that succeeded the Grecian kingdom have run their course, another king of fierce countenance emerges on the scene. This king will be responsible for the transgressions of humanity running rampant and out of control. The king of fierce countenance is the little horn (Dan. 8:9). The little horn is symbolic for Antichrist. He is the king that rejects the light of God and attempts to replace righteousness with darkness. His mentor is Satan, and his agenda is to install himself as the one and only god.

Dan. 8:24   And his power shall be mighty, but not by his own power: and he shall destroy wonderfully, and shall prosper, and practise, and shall destroy the mighty and the holy people.

Dan. 8:25   And through his policy also he shall cause craft to prosper in his hand; and he shall magnify himself in his heart, and by peace shall destroy many: he shall also stand up against the Prince of princes; but he shall be broken without hand.

In the last days, the Antichrist will wreak havoc on humanity. Everything seems to prosper in his hand. His power and authority is not a direct result of his great wisdom, but this nefarious king receives his seemingly unlimited authority from Satan (Rev. 13:2). He will abuse and destroy everything that is in opposition to his kingdom, especially the saints of the Lord.

He will display signs and wonders to deceive the saints into following him. He will magnify himself high above the Lord himself (2Th. 2:3–4). By peace, he will destroy a multitude of people (Dan. 9:27). He will also stand up against the followers of Jesus and blaspheme any and everything that's associated with the Lord. After his reign of terror surpasses the designated boundaries of the Lord, he will fall without any assistance from any of his fellow conspirators.

> Dan. 8:26   And the vision of the evening and the morning which was told is true: wherefore shut thou up the vision; for it shall be for many days.

This vision also references how long the Antichrist will continue to transgress against God's people (Dan. 8:13–14). During this time of trouble, the Antichrist will enact some groundbreaking new laws. The daily sacrifice (prayer) will become illegal. Anyone observed violating this law will be subject to the death penalty. Once enactment of this new law occurs, it will last until Christ's return.

This time of unprecedented trouble will continue for 2,300 days (Dan. 8:13–14). Please note, this is a reference to the Antichrist abolishing the daily sacrifice (prayer). The daily sacrifice occurred twice daily; once in the morning and once in the afternoon. A day consists of an evening and a morning sacrifice; therefore the 2,300 days are 2,300 times, which calculates to be 1,150 days. From the time that the daily sacrifice is enforced, there will be another 1,150 days before the Lord comes to cleanse the sanctuary and restore the daily sacrifice (prayer).

Daniel was instructed not to worry about the dream. Although the things in the dream will come to past, they are about end-time events.

These events would be many years in the future and would not come to fruition during Daniel's lifetime.

> Dan. 8:27   And I Daniel fainted, and was sick certain days; afterward I rose up, and did the king's business; and I was astonished at the vision, but none understood it.

After Gabriel finished giving the interpretation of the dream, Daniel fainted. He was sick for several days. After a brief recuperation period, Daniel regained his strength and returned to his duties. He was still preoccupied with the dream because he did not fully understand it.

CHAPTER 9

DANIEL'S PRAYER

Dan. 9:1	In the first year of Darius the son of Ahasuerus, of the seed of the Medes, which was made king over the realm of the Chaldeans;
Dan. 9:2	In the first year of his reign I Daniel understood by books the number of the years, whereof the word of the LORD came to Jeremiah the prophet, that he would accomplish seventy years in the desolations of Jerusalem.
Dan. 9:3	And I set my face unto the Lord God, to seek by prayer and supplications, with fasting, and sackcloth, and ashes:

Daniel Seeks Understanding

DANIEL is now living in the Medo-Persian kingdom. Darius the Mede is the king over the realm of the Chaldeans. Darius is the son of King Ahasuerus, and many scholars think Queen Esther is his mother. That being the case; he would be more sympathetic to the Hebrews.

Daniel understood the writings of Jeremiah concerning the number of years that Jerusalem will be under Babylonian captivity. Daniel is referencing the prophecy where Jeremiah prophesied Jerusalem would be under the authority of Babylon for seventy years (Jer. 25:11–12). He knew Jeremiah's prophesy was true because he had been a Babylonian captive for seventy years, and now Babylon has been overthrown by the Medo-Persians.

By all calculations, Daniel is eighty-plus years of age at this time. He is now living in the Medo-Persian kingdom, which succeeded the Babylonian kingdom. Daniel was in captivity for seventy years in the Babylonian kingdom. Assuming he was at least ten years old when he became a captive, that would make him at least eighty years old. Many scholars think Daniel died in captivity because there's no biblical record that he ever returned to his homeland.

Daniel understood the prophecy about seventy years of Babylonian captivity. He knows the seventy years is complete, but he wanted to understand the significance of his dreams in relationship to Jeremiah's prophesy of seventy years. Daniel could not make the connection; therefore, Daniel prepared himself with sackcloth and ashes to seek the Lord in prayer and supplication. He prayed for answers about the seventy years of Babylonian captivity and its connection to his dreams.

Daniel's Prayer

Dan. 9:4	And I prayed unto the LORD my God, and made my confession, and said, O Lord, the great and dreadful God, keeping the covenant and mercy to them that love him, and to them that keep his commandments;
Dan. 9:5	We have sinned, and have committed iniquity, and have done wickedly, and have rebelled, even by departing from thy precepts and from thy judgments:
Dan. 9:6	Neither have we hearkened unto thy servants the prophets, which spake in thy name to our kings, our princes, and our fathers, and to all the people of the land.
Dan. 9:7	O Lord, righteousness belongeth unto thee, but unto us confusion of faces, as at this day; to the men of Judah, and to the inhabitants of Jerusalem, and unto all Israel, that are near, and that are far off, through all the countries whither thou hast driven them, because of their trespass that they have trespassed against thee.
Dan. 9:8	O Lord, to us belongeth confusion of face, to our kings, to our princes, and to our fathers, because we have sinned against thee.

Dan. 9:9   To the Lord our God belong mercies and forgivenesses, though we have rebelled against him;

Dan. 9:10   Neither have we obeyed the voice of the LORD our God, to walk in his laws, which he set before us by his servants the prophets.

Dan. 9:11   Yea, all Israel have transgressed thy law, even by departing, that they might not obey thy voice; therefore the curse is poured upon us, and the oath that is written in the law of Moses the servant of God, because we have sinned against him.

Dan. 9:12   And he hath confirmed his words, which he spake against us, and against our judges that judged us, by bringing upon us a great evil: for under the whole heaven hath not been done as hath been done upon Jerusalem.

Dan. 9:13   As it is written in the law of Moses, all this evil is come upon us: yet made we not our prayer before the LORD our God, that we might turn from our iniquities, and understand thy truth.

Dan. 9:14   Therefore hath the LORD watched upon the evil, and brought it upon us: for the LORD our God is righteous in all his works which he doeth: for we obeyed not his voice.

Dan. 9:15   And now, O Lord our God, that hast brought thy people forth out of the land of Egypt with a mighty hand, and hast gotten thee renown, as at this day; we have sinned, we have done wickedly.

Dan. 9:16   O Lord, according to all thy righteousness, I beseech thee, let thine anger and thy fury be turned away from thy city Jerusalem, thy holy mountain: because for our sins, and for the iniquities of our fathers, Jerusalem and thy people are become a reproach to all that are about us.

Dan. 9:17   Now therefore, O our God, hear the prayer of thy servant, and his supplications, and cause thy face to shine upon thy sanctuary that is desolate, for the Lord's sake.

Dan. 9:18   O my God, incline thine ear, and hear; open thine eyes, and behold our desolations, and the city which is called by thy name: for we do not present our supplications before thee for our righteousnesses, but for thy great mercies.

Dan. 9:19   O Lord, hear; O Lord, forgive; O Lord, hearken and do; defer not, for thine own sake, O my God: for thy city and thy people are called by thy name.

Daniel 9:4–19 is the contents of Daniel's prayer. In his prayer, he acknowledges how great and mighty God is. He is the God that keeps covenant and mercy with anyone who loves him and keeps his commandments. He acknowledged that Israel had sinned and had committed iniquity. They had done wickedly and had rebelled by departing from the Lord's precepts and judgments. They refused to listen to the servants and prophets who spoke to their religious and political leaders in the name of the Lord.

The Lord is righteousness, but Israel had transgressed God's law by departing from the word that is written in the law of Moses. The Lord allowed all this evil to come upon Israel because the people did not pray before him for a change of heart. Repentance would have caused them to turn from their iniquities and understand his truth. Daniel acknowledged that the citizens of Jerusalem had become a reproach because of the sins and iniquities of their fathers. He knew the Lord is righteous, long-suffering, and forgiving. For that cause, he requested that the Lord let his anger and fury turn away from the people of Jerusalem.

Daniel then closed his prayer, asking the Lord to hear his prayer and to once again let his face shine upon his sanctuary for his name's sake and for the people that are called by his name, because the sanctuary was in a desolate state.

Daniel's Answered Prayer

Dan. 9:20   And whiles I was speaking, and praying, and confessing
             my sin and the sin of my people Israel, and presenting
             my supplication before the LORD my God for the holy
             mountain of my God;
Dan. 9:21   Yea, whiles I was speaking in prayer, even the man
             Gabriel, whom I had seen in the vision at the beginning,
             being caused to fly swiftly, touched me about the time of
             the evening oblation.
Dan. 9:22   And he informed me, and talked with me, and said,
             O Daniel, I am now come forth to give thee skill and
             understanding.
Dan. 9:23   At the beginning of thy supplications the command-
             ment came forth, and I am come to shew thee; for thou
             art greatly beloved: therefore understand the matter, and
             consider the vision.

Daniel was praying, confessing, and presenting his supplication to the Lord for himself and for the people of Israel. While he was still engaged in prayer, about 3:00 p.m., at the time of the second daily prayer, Gabriel the archangel appeared from nowhere. Daniel recognized him because he had seen him before in his second dream (Dan. 8:16–17). Gabriel reached over and touched Daniel and began to converse with him. Gabriel explained to Daniel that he is well respected in heaven, and God dispatched him as soon as he started praying. The purpose of his visitation was to provide Daniel with answers to his prayer and impart wisdom concerning his dreams.

Daniel's Seventy Weeks

Dan. 9:24   Seventy weeks are determined upon thy people and
             upon thy holy city, to finish the transgression, and to
             make an end of sins, and to make reconciliation for iniq-
             uity, and to bring in everlasting righteousness, and to seal
             up the vision and prophecy, and to anoint the most Holy.
Dan. 9:25   Know therefore and understand, that from the going
             forth of the commandment to restore and to build
             Jerusalem unto the Messiah the Prince shall be seven
             weeks, and threescore and two weeks: the street shall be
             built again, and the wall, even in troublous times.

Many scholars reference the following verses of this chapter, as
Daniel's Seventy Weeks. Gabriel has just appeared on the scene, and he
made it clear to Daniel that he was there to give him understanding about
his dreams. Somehow Daniel thought he was there to give him clarity about
what will happen after the seventy years of Babylonian captivity. After all,
the seventy years of captivity was complete, and the reigning Medo-Persian
kingdom had already overthrown the Babylonian kingdom.

It is apparent that Daniel and Gabriel are referencing two different
prophecies concerning *seventy*. Daniel is referencing seventy years of
Babylonian captivity (Jer. 25:11–12). Gabriel is referencing seventy weeks
of Israel's future history. Daniel was ignorant of the fact that his dreams
were about Israel's future. Although Gabriel had previously provided
Daniel with this information, he failed to connect the dots (Dan. 8:16–17).

The seventy weeks of Babylonian captivity was really about the land
of Israel enjoying her Sabbaths (Lev. 25:3–4). The people of Israel failed
to allow for the land of Israel to lie dormant every seven years, thereby
depriving the land of her Sabbaths. The land of Israel did get to enjoy her
Sabbaths many years later. She got to enjoy her Sabbaths while Israel was
exiled into the Babylonian captivity for seventy years (Lev. 26:34).

The seventy weeks of Gabriel's prophecy was about God's direct involvement with the nation of Israel (Dan. 9:24). God will be dealing directly with the people of Israel and Jerusalem, the holy city. This intervention is a period when the Lord will finish the transgressions of the people of Israel and make an end of sins. The Lord will make reconciliation for their iniquity, bringing in everlasting righteousness and anointing the Messiah.

Gabriel is talking about seventy weeks that sums up the entire history of the nation of Israel. The Seventy Weeks will begin when the commandment to restore and rebuild Jerusalem is given, and it will extend up to and include the end-time. Gabriel continues with more detail. From the going forth of the commandment to restore and rebuild Jerusalem for the Messiah, the prince; there will be seven weeks and sixty-two weeks, which is a total of sixty-nine weeks. This is one week short of the seventy weeks of which Gabriel spoke.

Daniel 9:24 references seventy weeks. Before we continue, the word *weeks* must be qualified. Please note, from man's perspective, seventy weeks are seventy periods of seven days. The Hebrew word for weeks does not necessarily mean seven days. The Hebrew word for week is *shabuwa* #H7620 that means seven. It can be seven of anything. It does not always mean seven weeks or seven years. It could be seven weeks, seven hours, seven minutes, seven years, seven months, seven babies, seven days, seven men, seven women, seven cars, seven dogs, and so forth. What the Hebrew seven is referencing depends on how it is used in the contents. One example of the utilization of the Hebrew seven is in the book of Genesis. Jacob is instructed to fulfill Rachel's week (Gen. 29:27). Jacob served Laban for an additional week (seven years). In this verse, the expression (fulfill her week) means *seven years*. Ezekiel 45:21 is an example where seven is referencing days. Exodus 2:16 is another example where seven is referencing daughters.

Concerning Daniel's Seventy Weeks, and how the word *seven* is used, we must look at the contents and scripture reference. Look at the order of events concerning the rebuilding of the temple. The decree was given to rebuild Jerusalem (Ezr. 5:13). It took about seven weeks for the rebuilding to be completed (Neh. 2:1–10). Scripture states that it took forty-six years to rebuild the temple (Joh. 2:20). Doing the math, seven times seven equals forty-nine. Scripture states, the construction of Jerusalem ceased until the second year of Darius. This stoppage in construction accounts for two years. Perhaps the other year was under Artaxerxes's reign when he ordered the rebuilding project to cease (Ezr. 2:23–24). We can conclude that the Hebrew word for weeks in this passage is referencing *years*.

King Cyrus gave the commandment to begin the rebuilding of Jerusalem (Ezr. 1:1–11). The rebuilding took about seven weeks (forty-nine years). During the rebuilding phase of Jerusalem, the construction crew encountered much opposition (Neh. 4:1–23). The rebuilding of Jerusalem was finally completed in the sixth year of Darius' reign (Ezr. 6:14).

Dan. 9:26   And after threescore and two weeks shall Messiah be cut off, but not for himself: and the people of the prince that shall come shall destroy the city and the sanctuary; and the end thereof shall be with a flood, and unto the end of the war desolations are determined.

Dan. 9:27   And he shall confirm the covenant with many for one week: and in the midst of the week he shall cause the sacrifice and the oblation to cease, and for the overspreading of abominations he shall make it desolate, even until the consummation, and that determined shall be poured upon the desolate.

After the completion of the rebuilding of Jerusalem, there was another period of sixty-two weeks (434 years) before the crucifixion of Messiah. This only accounts for sixty-nine weeks (483 years). Gabriel continued to speak about a time of desolations that will usher in the destruction of the city of Jerusalem and the sanctuary. This time of desolations is what many scholars reference as Daniel's Seventieth Week (a seven-year period).

The final week (seven years) begins with a seven-year covenant between Israel and the Antichrist (Dan. 9:27). One of the stipulations of the agreement is that there will be some much-needed peace. That peace is short-lived because the Antichrist will violate the treaty in three and a half years. During the last half of the covenant, Antichrist will wreak havoc on the nation of Israel. He will abolish the daily sacrifice (daily prayer), and he will initiate the Abomination of Desolation, which causes many people to commit the unpardonable sin. The implementation of the abomination of desolation is also confirmed in the New Testament (Mat. 24:15).

Usually, when someone speaks of Daniel's Seventy Weeks, they are referencing 490 years (seventy weeks of years). We know this prophecy took place over 2,500 years ago; therefore, we must be missing the correct interpretation or meaning because more than 490 years has passed since the command went forth to rebuild Jerusalem. Daniel misunderstood the prophecy, too. He thought it was about the completion of the seventy years of Babylonian captivity. Gabriel made it very clear—the prophecy was about ending sin and bringing in everlasting righteousness.

Gabriel stated that it would take seven weeks (of years) to restore and rebuild Jerusalem (7 * 7 = 49 years). It will take another sixty-two weeks for Messiah to be cut off (7 * 62 = 434 years). From the time they begin to rebuild Jerusalem and Messiah is cut off, is a total of 483 years; 49 + 434 = 483 yrs. We know more than 483 years has passed since this rebuilding project began. We also know that there is still sin in the world, and we are not experiencing everlasting righteousness. What are we missing?

The Messiah was cut off (crucified) after sixty-nine weeks (483 years) had passed from the commandment to rebuild Jerusalem. We have only accounted for sixty-nine weeks. There is one week (7 years) left. Daniel 9:27 accounts for that one last week, but there's still a problem. We know for a fact that sin did not end, and everlasting righteousness still does not exist. We also know that more than seven years have passed since the death, burial, resurrection, and ascension of Jesus Christ. How can we explain this?

The answer to this question is that there was a break in time. When Christ was cut off (crucified), the time stopped for Israel. Jesus' crucifixion was the beginning of the New Covenant. From the death of Christ to now is more than seven years. This period is when God was not dealing only with the Jews. He was dealing with the Gentiles as he was establishing the church. This period is known as the times of the Gentiles. The following verses are references to the times of the Gentiles:

Luk. 21:24   And they shall fall by the edge of the sword, and shall be led away captive into all nations: and Jerusalem shall be trodden down of the Gentiles, until the times of the Gentiles be fulfilled.

Rom. 11:25   For I would not, brethren, that ye should be ignorant of this mystery, lest ye should be wise in your own conceits; that blindness in part is happened to Israel, until the fulness of the Gentiles be come in.

Rom. 10:19   But I say, Did not Israel know? First Moses saith, I will provoke you to jealousy by them that are no people, and by a foolish nation I will anger you.

Rom. 11:11   I say then, Have they stumbled that they should fall? God forbid: but rather through their fall salvation is come unto the Gentiles, for to provoke them to jealousy.

There were a total of sixty-nine weeks before the crucifixion of Christ. That period of sixty-nine weeks consists of two parts; a seven-week period (49 years), and a sixty-two-week period (434 years). That was a total of 483 years, so there is one week (7 years) remaining. There was a break in time with the death of the Messiah, and it will continue when Antichrist emerges and signs a one-week (7 year) treaty with Israel. Christ died around AD 30. Counting backward, King Cyrus gave the commandment to restore and rebuild Jerusalem at approximately 453 BC.

There was a stoppage of the rebuilding of Jerusalem by King Artaxerxes (Ezr. 4:17–24). Later King Darius gave the order to continue the restoration of Jerusalem (Ezr. 4:24). King Darius is probably the son of King Ahasuerus and Queen Ester. If Darius was in fact of Hebrew ancestry, that could have influenced his decision to continue to restore and rebuild Jerusalem. The restoration of Jerusalem was completed in the sixth year of King Darius (Ezr. 6:15).

Israel and Antichrist will ratify a one-week (7 year) covenant. This period is often called the seven-year tribulation period. In the middle of that week, Antichrist causes the sacrifice and oblation to cease (praise and worship). Being forbidden to praise and worship freely is one reason many refer to the last three and a half years of the seven years covenant as the great tribulation.

The seventy weeks recorded in the book of Daniel is referencing the amount of time (prophetically) that God deals directly with Israel before his return. Please note, there was an intermission after sixty-nine weeks (483 years) was completed. The final week (7 years) will resume with the signing of a seven-year covenant between Antichrist and Israel.

.

CHAPTER 10

THE HEAVENLY BEING

Dan. 10:1 In the third year of Cyrus king of Persia a thing
was revealed unto Daniel, whose name was called
Belteshazzar; and the thing was true, but the time
appointed was long: and he understood the thing, and
had understanding of the vision.

Dan. 10:2 In those days I Daniel was mourning three full weeks.

Dan. 10:3 I ate no pleasant bread, neither came flesh nor wine in
my mouth, neither did I anoint myself at all, till three
whole weeks were fulfilled.

The Importance of Fasting

WHILE in Babylonian captivity, Daniel's name was changed to
Belteshazzar (Dan. 1:7). Now he's under the authority of the
Medo-Persian Kingdom and he's still meditating on the dreams of King
Nebuchadnezzar. It was the third year of Cyrus, king of Persia. Daniel
had been fasting for three weeks, during which he abstained from eating
any meat or drinking any wine. While he was fasting, he had a revelation.
Scripture does not disclose the contents of the revelation, but perhaps it
pertained to end-time events.

This time, he better understood the revelation because he possessed
knowledge and understanding of dreams and visions. He knew the revelation would come to pass, but he also realized it was a long way off
because it was a future prophecy. Perhaps he was connecting the dots with
his knowledge of Nebuchadnezzar's dreams. In Daniel chapter 2, King
Nebuchadnezzar had a dream about a great image. The image referenced

future events and it gave Daniel a glance into the future about coming kingdoms. Daniel is praying and fasting to gain more insight about the future. Many people make the mistake of thinking Daniel is seeking answers about the seventy weeks, simply because Gabriel mentioned it in the preceding chapter. Please note the chronological order of the events recorded in the book of Daniel. Please see Appendix A. Chapter 10 follows immediately after chapter 4. For that reason, Daniel could not be seeking clarity about the seventy weeks, because Gabriel had not spoken to him at this time.

Daniel was a man of God. He prayed three times a day (Dan. 6:10). Daniel prayed when his understanding of a matter evaded him. When Daniel received his final recorded revelation, he was confused about its meaning. He knew the revelation was futuristic, but he wanted more clarity. He began to seek the Lord for answers by fasting and prayer. Daniel probably clothed himself with sackcloth and ashes as he had dressed in times past when seeking the Lord for answers (Dan. 9:3). He prayed without ceasing for twenty-one days. He was such a humble man that he even refused to anoint himself while he sought the Lord for answers.

Dan. 10:4   And in the four and twentieth day of the first month, as I was by the side of the great river, which is Hiddekel;

Dan. 10:5   Then I lifted up mine eyes, and looked, and behold a certain man clothed in linen, whose loins were girded with fine gold of Uphaz:

Dan. 10:6   His body also was like the beryl, and his face as the appearance of lightning, and his eyes as lamps of fire, and his arms and his feet like in colour to polished brass, and the voice of his words like the voice of a multitude.

In the twenty-fourth day of the first month, Daniel was by the side of the great Hiddekel River. This river is the third river that emptied from the Garden of Eden (Gen. 2:14). Another name for the Hiddekel River is the Tigris River. Daniel was fasting and seeking the Lord when he lifted his eyes because something strange caught his attention. He saw a man clothed in linen; his loins girded with fine gold of Uphaz; his body also was like the beryl, his face as the appearance of lightning, his eyes as lamps of fire, and his arms and his feet were the color of polished brass. When the man spoke, his words sounded like the voice of a multitude. The sound of the man's voice is synonymous with the voice John heard when he received his revelation (Rev. 19:6).

Perhaps the certain man that Daniel saw was Gabriel. In Daniel 7:16, Daniel asked someone to give him the interpretation of his first dream. In Daniel 8:16, Gabriel is instructed to give Daniel the interpretation of his second dream. In Daniel 9:21, it is Gabriel that reveals to Daniel the prophecy of the seventy weeks. Daniel also identifies Gabriel as the man that he saw in his first dream. Another telling sign that the man is Gabriel is because he kept company with Michael, who is another archangel (Dan. 10:13). Please note, the description of the man in Daniel 10:4–6, parallels with the description of the man in Revelation 1:13–16.

Dan. 10:7   And I Daniel alone saw the vision: for the men that were with me saw not the vision; but a great quaking fell upon them, so that they fled to hide themselves.

Dan. 10:8   Therefore I was left alone, and saw this great vision, and there remained no strength in me: for my comeliness was turned in me into corruption, and I retained no strength.

Dan. 10:9   Yet heard I the voice of his words: and when I heard the voice of his words, then was I in a deep sleep on my face, and my face toward the ground.

Daniel was with a group of men by the Hiddekel River. Scripture doesn't disclose why they had gathered; perhaps they were engaging in corporate prayer. Only Daniel saw the man (Gabriel). The men that were with him did not see him, but they did experience a quaking of the ground. Not knowing what was happening, they fled for safety. Perhaps the quaking of the earth occurred when Gabriel began to speak. This scenario is synonymous with the children of Israel when God began to speak to them; the ground also quaked (Exo. 19:18).

When Daniel's entourage fled the scene because of fear, Daniel was left alone. He became very weak, and his body appeared to be lifeless. Daniel fainted upon hearing Gabriel's voice. He had the same response that John experienced when he encountered someone with the same description, revealing future events to him (Rev. 1:13–17).

Dan. 10:10   And, behold, an hand touched me, which set me upon my knees and upon the palms of my hands.

Dan. 10:11   And he said unto me, O Daniel, a man greatly beloved, understand the words that I speak unto thee, and stand upright: for unto thee am I now sent. And when he had spoken this word unto me, I stood trembling.

Dan. 10:12   Then said he unto me, Fear not, Daniel: for from the first day that thou didst set thine heart to understand, and to chasten thyself before thy God, thy words were heard, and I am come for thy words.

Dan. 10:13   But the prince of the kingdom of Persia withstood me one and twenty days: but, lo, Michael, one of the chief princes, came to help me; and I remained there with the kings of Persia.

Dan. 10:14   Now I am come to make thee understand what shall befall thy people in the latter days: for yet the vision is for many days.

When Gabriel began to speak to Daniel, he fainted. Immediately, Daniel felt a hand touch him and strengthened him so that he could rise on his hands and knees. Gabriel continued by commanding Daniel to stand on his feet. Then he began to disclose to him the purpose for his visit. Daniel was able to muster enough strength to stand upright, although he was still trembling.

Gabriel continued to assure him that he had nothing to fear. He was there because Daniel had prayed and God heard his prayer. God sent him to explain the meaning of all the dreams, visions, and revelations. He informs Daniel that the Lord dispatched him the very first day that he began fasting and praying to seek the Lord for answers, but another spiritual entity detained him. The heavenly being that was in charge of Persia detained him for twenty-one days. Michael the archangel came to his assistance so that he could continue on his journey. Now that he has arrived, he can disclose to him, the things that await the people of Israel in the latter days. He's revealing the information now, but the manifestation of it is many days in the future.

Dan. 10:15   And when he had spoken such words unto me, I set my face toward the ground, and I became dumb.

Dan. 10:16   And, behold, one like the similitude of the sons of men touched my lips: then I opened my mouth, and spake, and said unto him that stood before me, O my lord, by the vision my sorrows are turned upon me, and I have retained no strength.

Dan. 10:17   For how can the servant of this my lord talk with this my lord? for as for me, straightway there remained no strength in me, neither is there breath left in me.

Dan. 10:18   Then there came again and touched me one like the appearance of a man, and he strengthened me,

Dan. 10:19   And said, O man greatly beloved, fear not: peace be unto thee, be strong, yea, be strong. And when he had spoken unto me, I was strengthened, and said, Let my lord speak; for thou hast strengthened me.

When Gabriel had spoken these words to Daniel, he became so weak that he could not hold up his head or speak a word. It was like all of the life had been drained from his body. Gabriel reached out and touched his lips, causing him to regain his composure. At that point, Daniel began to question himself. He asked, "How can he, who cannot even speak when in the presence of a servant of the Lord, be of any service to the Lord?"

Gabriel touched Daniel again to strengthen him. He again assured Daniel that he should be empowered and not fear because heaven loves his diligence and faithfulness. Immediately, Daniel received a burst of energy, and he was ready to receive Gabriel's message.

> Dan. 10:20   Then said he, Knowest thou wherefore I come unto thee? and now will I return to fight with the prince of Persia: and when I am gone forth, lo, the prince of Grecia shall come.
>
> Dan. 10:21   But I will shew thee that which is noted in the scripture of truth: and there is none that holdeth with me in these things, but Michael your prince.

Gabriel explains to Daniel, the purpose for his visit. He's there to reveal to him things that are already written in scripture. Those things are about future events. They are true. They will come to pass, and he's there to give him understanding with clarity. He also informs Daniel that this information is on a need-to-know basis; only Michael and he were privy to that information.

Gabriel informed Daniel that after he finish revealing to him the things that will befall Israel in the last days, he was going to return to fight with the prince of Persia. After he finished fighting with the prince of Persia, another prince would arrive on the scene. The new prince that will follow, is the prince of Greece. The reference to another prince arriving on the scene is a reference to the fall of the Medo-Persian kingdom and the kingdom of Greece rising to power.

This visit by Gabriel is during the Medo-Persian kingdom. Michael and Gabriel are archangels, and the princes of Persia and Grecia are angelic beings. Michael and Gabriel are engaged in a spiritual war against the prince of Persia. Although it is a spiritual war, it has physical consequences. Because these battles are spiritual warfare, it brings to mind two

New Testament scriptures. Ephesians 2:2 states, "Wherein in time past ye walked according to the course of this world, according to the prince of the power of the air, the spirit that now worketh in the children of disobedience." Ephesians 6:12 states, "For we wrestle not against flesh and blood, but against principalities, against powers, against the rulers of the darkness of this world, against spiritual wickedness in high places."

THE KINGDOM'S EXPLOITS

Dan. 11:1   Also I in the first year of Darius the Mede, even I, stood
              to confirm and to strengthen him.

Exploits of the Kingdoms

CHAPTER 11 is a continuation of chapter 9. Please note, the book of Daniel isn't written in chronological order. Chapters 9 and 11 occurs in the first year of the reign of King Darius and chapter 10 occurs in the third year of the reign of King Cyrus. This chapter is the interpretation of the different visions that Daniel and Nebuchadnezzar dreamed. The setting is in the Medo-Persian kingdom with King Darius of the Medes.

Gabriel is speaking, and he informs Daniel that when Darius the Mede took office, he (Gabriel) was there to strengthen him (Daniel). Gabriel is a spiritual being, fighting spiritual battles. Note: there is spiritual wickedness in high places (Eph. 6:12). Gabriel is explaining to Daniel what will happen in the latter days. He even told Daniel that after he finished talking with him, he would return to fight against the prince of Persia (Dan. 10:13; 10:20).

Daniel chapter 11, from verses 1 to verse 30 is an account of world history. It is so accurate that many scholars believe that someone wrote the book of Daniel after the fact. Bear in mind; this is a prophecy that came directly from the Lord himself. God knows the beginning from the ending, so he gave us a preview of historical events. Note the events of this prophecy were future to Daniel, and at the same time they are historical facts to those of us living today. Only God could have provided such precision and detail in advance.

Dan. 11:2   And now will I shew thee the truth. Behold, there
shall stand up yet three kings in Persia; and the fourth
shall be far richer than they all: and by his strength
through his riches he shall stir up all against the realm
of Grecia.

Gabriel is revealing to Daniel the truth about the different dreams and
visions, experienced by Nebuchadnezzar and Daniel. Remember the image
that Nebuchadnezzar dreamed about represents four world kingdoms
(Dan. 2:29–44), and the four beasts that Daniel dreamed about respectively
represent the same four world kingdoms (Dan. 7:1–17). The head of gold
(Dan. 2:38) and the first beast (Dan. 7:4) are symbolic for the Babylonian
kingdom.

Daniel 7:4 describe the first beast (Babylonian kingdom) as having the
appearance of a lion with two wings on its back. The significance of the
lion having two wings on its back is that *wings* are symbolic for a specific
reign or period. Although the Babylonian kingdom (lion) had one head,
it had two distinct periods of power. The first wing is symbolic for King
Nebuchadnezzar, and the second wing is symbolic for King Belshazzar;
both of them are from the Babylonian kingdom.

The Babylonian kingdom ceased to exist with the death of Belshazzar
(Dan. 5:30–31). The Medes and Persians came into power after the fall of
Babylon. There will be a total of three kings of Persia. They are Cyrus,
Darius, and Artaxerxes (Ezr. 6:14). Although there are more Persian kings,
these three had direct dealings with the domination of the nation of Israel.
After the destruction of the Medo-Persian kingdom, there would arise a
third leader who would be wealthy and powerful, and he would intimidate
the surrounding nations.

Daniel 7:5 describe the second beast (Medo-Persian kingdom) as
having the likeness of a bear. The Medo-Persian kingdom is the kingdom
that corresponds with or is equivalent to the silver breast and silver arms of

the image in Nebuchadnezzar's first dream (Dan. 2:32). The Medo-Persian kingdom with its vast military power began to set its sights on the Grecians.

> Dan. 11:3   And a mighty king shall stand up, that shall rule with great dominion, and do according to his will.

When the Medo-Persian kingdom fells, a mighty kingdom would succeed it. The name of the successor kingdom is the Grecian kingdom (Dan. 8:21; 10:20). The Grecian kingdom would be powerful, and it would rule with great dominion. It would conquer and destroy its enemies at will. The leader of the Grecian Kingdom was Alexander the Great.

> Dan. 11:4   And when he shall stand up, his kingdom shall be broken, and shall be divided toward the four winds of heaven; and not to his posterity, nor according to his dominion which he ruled: for his kingdom shall be plucked up, even for others beside those.

Daniel 7:6 describes the third beast as having the appearance of a leopard with four heads and four wings on its back. The four heads are symbolic for four separate kingdoms, and the four wings are symbolic for four specific reigns or time periods. Each of the four heads corresponds to its respective wing.

Alexander the Great died at a young age, and his death initiated the death of the Grecian kingdom. The kingdom underwent divisions into four lesser kingdoms. The beast (leopard) is the Grecian kingdom, headed by Alexander the Great. The four heads are four different lesser kingdoms. The four wings are four specific reigns or time periods. Each of the four lesser kingdoms is equivalent to one head and one wing of the leopard (Grecian Kingdom). The division of the four new kingdoms took on the compass designation as kings of the north, south, east, and west, respectively.

The northern kingdom was the Syrian kingdom, and the Seleucid family controlled it. The southern kingdom was the Egyptian kingdom, and the Ptolemy family controlled it. According to history, the western kingdom was the Macedonian kingdom, controlled by General Cassander. The eastern kingdom was the kingdom of Thrace, controlled by General Lysimachus.

Daniel 8:8 describes a male goat with one horn. The leopard in chapter 7 and the one-horned male goat in chapter 8 are synonymous. The goat with one horn symbolizes the Grecian kingdom of which Alexander the Great is king. The breakage of the one horn initiates the growth of four smaller horns. The Grecian kingdom split into four parts, but Alexander the Great's relatives did not inherit any of those divisions. The kingdom was distributed between Alexander the Great's four generals.

> Dan. 11:5   And the king of the south shall be strong, and one of his princes; and he shall be strong above him, and have dominion; his dominion shall be a great dominion.

Daniel 11:15–30 tells of the history of the next two kingdoms to rule and reign over Israel, after the division of the Grecian kingdom. These are two of the four kingdoms that derived from the division of the Grecian kingdom. Scripture references them as the king of the north and the king of the south. The king of the north is the Syrian kingdom, and the king of the south is the Egyptian kingdom. The Seleucid family ruled the Syrian kingdom, and the Ptolemy family ruled the Egyptian kingdom.

The symbolism for the northern kingdom and the southern kingdom is the two legs of iron of the image in Nebuchadnezzar's dream (Dan. 2:33). Just as two legs stand side by side, these two kingdoms existed with exuberant power during the same period.

The Syrian and Egyptian kingdoms are referenced as the first and second head and first and second wing of the leopard with four heads and four wings in Daniel's first dream (Dan. 7:6). They are also referenced as the first and second horns of the four notable horns in Daniel's second dream (Dan. 8:8).

From history, we know that there were many battles fought between the North (Syria) and the South (Egypt). These kingdoms fought back and forth for years. At one point, the King of the South was Ptolemy Soter, and he chose one prince (son) over the other. He favored Ptolemy Philadelphus over Ptolemy Keraunos, his other son. Ptolemy Keraunos went north and became confederate with his father's enemies.

> Dan. 11:6   And in the end of years they shall join themselves together; for the king's daughter of the south shall come to the king of the north to make an agreement: but she shall not retain the power of the arm; neither shall he stand, nor his arm: but she shall be given up, and they that brought her, and he that begat her, and he that strengthened her in these times.

After many years of infighting, there was a marriage arrangement between the daughter of the king of the south (Egypt) and the son of the king of the north (Syria). The underlying purpose of this marriage arrangement was to strengthen their armies.

There was also some betrayal between these two kingdoms. According to history, Berenice was the daughter of Ptolemy II Philadelphus. She became the wife of the Seleucid monarch, Antiochus II Theos. He was already married to Laodice. Under the agreement, he divorced his wife Laodice and transferred the succession to Berenice's children. After Ptolemy II Philadelphus (south) died, Antiochus II Theos (north) repudiated Berenice and took back Laodice. Immediately Laodice poisoned Antiochus II Theos and murdered Berenice and her son.[10]

> Dan. 11:7   But out of a branch of her roots shall one stand up in

---

[10] *The New Oxford Annotated Bible* (Oxford University Press, 2001), [1274 Hebrew Bible].

his estate, which shall come with an army, and shall enter into the fortress of the king of the north, and shall deal against them, and shall prevail:

One of Ptolemy II Phidalelphus's sons, Ptolemy III Euergetes, wanted revenge because of the murder of his sister Berenice. He led an army against the king of the north, Seleucus II Callinicus.[11]

Dan. 11:8   And shall also carry captives into Egypt their gods, with their princes, and with their precious vessels of silver and of gold; and he shall continue more years than the king of the north.

Dan. 11:9   So the king of the south shall come into his kingdom, and shall return into his own land.

Referencing verse 7, the King of the South, Ptolemy III Euergetes, defeated the King of the North, Seleucus II Callinicus. He was then very strong, and he continued to rule for many years. After defeating the Syrians, Ptolemy III Euergetes took many spoils back to Egypt. He took captives, their gods, their princes, and their precious vessels made of silver and gold.[12]

Dan. 11:10   But his sons shall be stirred up, and shall assemble a multitude of great forces: and one shall certainly come, and overflow, and pass through: then shall he return, and be stirred up, even to his fortress.

Seleucus II Callinicus was the King of the North (Syria). His sons sought revenge when Ptolemy III Euergetes of Egypt defeated Syria. His

---

[11] *The New Oxford Annotated Bible* (Oxford University Press, 2001), [1274 Hebrew Bible].

[12] *The New Oxford Annotated Bible* (Oxford University Press, 2001), [1274 Hebrew Bible].

son's names were Seleucus III Ceraunus and Antiochus III the Great.[13] Seleucus III Ceraunus is also known as Seleucus III Sotor, and he invaded the King of the South.

> Dan. 11:11 And the king of the south shall be moved with choler, and shall come forth and fight with him, even with the king of the north: and he shall set forth a great multitude; but the multitude shall be given into his hand.
>
> Dan. 11:12 And when he hath taken away the multitude, his heart shall be lifted up; and he shall cast down many ten thousands: but he shall not be strengthened by it.

Ptolemy IV Philopater is the son of Ptolemy III Euergetes of Egypt. He was very angry with the king of the north (Syria), so he mounted an offense against Antiochus III the Great, the king of the north. The king of the south (Ptolemy IV Philopater) defeated the king of the north (Antiochus III the Great) in the Battle of Raphia.[14] After his victory, he became very prideful, and that pride affected his judgment. He became so unstable that he began to overthrow many of his countrymen. Such actions caused his popularity to dwindle in the polls.

> Dan. 11:13 For the king of the north shall return, and shall set forth a multitude greater than the former, and shall certainly come after certain years with a great army and with much riches.
>
> Dan. 11:14 And in those times there shall many stand up against the king of the south: also the robbers of thy people shall exalt themselves to establish the vision; but they shall fall.

---

[13] *The New Oxford Annotated Bible* (Oxford University Press, 2001), [1275 Hebrew Bible].

[14] *The New Oxford Annotated Bible* (Oxford University Press, 2001), (1275 Hebrew Bible].

Dan. 11:15   So the king of the north shall come, and cast up a mount, and take the most fenced cities: and the arms of the south shall not withstand, neither his chosen people, neither shall there be any strength to withstand.

Dan. 11:16   But he that cometh against him shall do according to his own will, and none shall stand before him: and he shall stand in the glorious land, which by his hand shall be consumed.

Dan. 11:17   He shall also set his face to enter with the strength of his whole kingdom, and upright ones with him; thus shall he do: and he shall give him the daughter of women, corrupting her: but she shall not stand on his side, neither be for him.

Dan. 11:18   After this shall he turn his face unto the isles, and shall take many: but a prince for his own behalf shall cause the reproach offered by him to cease; without his own reproach he shall cause it to turn upon him.

Dan. 11:19   Then he shall turn his face toward the fort of his own land: but he shall stumble and fall, and not be found.

After the defeat at the Battle of Raphia, the king of the north (Antiochus III the Great) gathered a greater army than the previous one. He returned to Egypt with greater wealth and a better-equipped army. Ptolemy IV Philopater tried to mount an offense, but because he previously overthrew some of his countrymen, that resistance failed. The king of the North captured the most fortified cities of the Southern kingdom. Antiochus III the Great was so powerful that he did whatever he chose to do. He entered into the glorious land (Israel), and he consumed it.[15]

Antiochus III the Great gave his daughter, Cleopatra I of Syria, to Ptolemy V Epiphanes of Egypt, to be his wife. This union was another marriage arrangement that was supposed to ensure peace. Antiochus III the Great of Syria was so confident his daughter's marriage would establish

---

[15] *The Jewish Study Bible* (Oxford University Press, 2004), 1663.

peace that he turned to conquer some of the islands off the coast. His daughter, Cleopatra I, sided with her Egyptian husband and turned against her father. Because of his daughter's betrayal, he decided to return home where he died. It is not clear how he died.[16]

> Dan. 11:20   Then shall stand up in his estate a raiser of taxes in the glory of the kingdom: but within few days he shall be destroyed, neither in anger, nor in battle.

Seleucus IV Philopater of Syria, who succeeded Antiochus III, sent Heliodorus to rob Jerusalem's temple treasury. This attempt was unsuccessful because a divine apparition chastised Heliodorus, ensuring his defeat, was not initiated by wrath or by war.[17]

> Dan. 11:21   And in his estate shall stand up a vile person, to whom they shall not give the honour of the kingdom: but he shall come in peaceably, and obtain the kingdom by flatteries.
> Dan. 11:22   And with the arms of a flood shall they be overflown from before him, and shall be broken; yea, also the prince of the covenant.
> Dan. 11:23   And after the league made with him he shall work deceitfully: for he shall come up, and shall become strong with a small people.
> Dan. 11:24   He shall enter peaceably even upon the fattest places of the province; and he shall do that which his fathers have not done, nor his fathers' fathers; he shall scatter among them the prey, and spoil, and riches: yea, and he shall forecast his devices against the strong holds, even for a time.

---

[16] *The Jewish Study Bible* (Oxford University Press, 2004), 1663.
[17] *The Jewish Study Bible* (Oxford University Press, 2004), 1663.

Antiochus IV Epiphanes of Syria was the successor to Seleucus IV Philopater. The books of the Maccabees give tons of information about Antiochus IV Epiphanes of Syria. He deceitfully spoke peaceable words to the people of Israel, and they believed him. Then he suddenly turned on the city and dealt it a severe blow, causing the destruction of many people (1 Mac. 1:30). Antiochus IV Epiphanes also installed a man named Jason into the office of high priest by corruption (2 Mac. 4:7–10). He did abominable acts by changing the laws and customs (1 Mac. 1:44–50). He erected a desolating sacrilege to challenge the religious beliefs of Israel (1 Mac. 1:54–57).

Antiochus IV Epiphanes was a vile person. He required Eleazar, a ninety-year-old scribe, to defile his religion by eating swine's flesh. He refused to eat the flesh of a swine, but the guards had compassion and told him to pretend to eat it. Again, he refused to even pretend to eat it. Instead, he welcomed death (2 Mac 6:18–20). Antiochus IV Epiphanes was also responsible for the execution of a mother and her seven sons in a horrific fashion (2 Mac. 7:1–42).

Dan. 11:25   And he shall stir up his power and his courage against the king of the south with a great army; and the king of the south shall be stirred up to battle with a very great and mighty army; but he shall not stand: for they shall forecast devices against him.

Dan. 11:26   Yea, they that feed of the portion of his meat shall destroy him, and his army shall overflow: and many shall fall down slain.

Dan. 11:27   And both these kings' hearts shall be to do mischief, and they shall speak lies at one table; but it shall not prosper: for yet the end shall be at the time appointed.

Dan. 11:28   Then shall he return into his land with great riches; and his heart shall be against the holy covenant; and he shall do exploits, and return to his own land.

The wars between the Syrians and Egyptians continued. There were two Egyptian stewards who had cultivated a special bond with Antiochus IV Epiphanes, and they plotted against him. They thought the Egyptian military was far superior to the Syrian military, so they encouraged Antiochus IV Epiphanes to invade Egypt. The Syrians soon thwarted the steward's expectation of an Egyptian victory.[18]

Dan. 11:29   At the time appointed he shall return, and come toward the south; but it shall not be as the former, or as the latter.

Dan. 11:30   For the ships of Chittim shall come against him: therefore he shall be grieved, and return, and have indignation against the holy covenant: so shall he do; he shall even return, and have intelligence with them that forsake the holy covenant.

After some time passed, the king of the North (Antiochus IV Epiphanes) attacked the king of the South (Egypt). The ships of Chittim (Rome) came to the aid of the South and forced the Syrians to withdraw from Egypt.

Many years later, after the rise and fall of many kings of the Syrian and Egyptian empires, Syria and Egypt were overthrown. According to history, Syria and Egypt became Roman provinces at approximately 50 BC. Their overthrow was the birth of another kingdom: the Roman Empire or the Macedonian Empire.

The Roman Empire (Macedonian kingdom) is the third head and third wing on the back of the leopard (Dan. 7:6). The Roman Empire is also the third horn of the four horns that sprouted up after the goat's one horn was broken (Dan. 8:8). The third head and third wing on the back of the leopard is synonymous with the third horn that replaced the broken horn of the goat (Dan. 8:8). Both are referencing the Macedonian kingdom or

---

[18] *The New Oxford Annotated Bible* (Oxford University Press, 2001), [1275–1276 Hebrew Bible].

Roman Empire, which are synonymous with the feet made of iron and clay of Nebuchadnezzar's image (Dan. 2:33). The Roman Empire is the western kingdom that was established after the division of the Grecian kingdom into four counterparts.

> Dan. 11:31   And arms shall stand on his part, and they shall pollute the sanctuary of strength, and shall take away the daily sacrifice, and they shall place the abomination that maketh desolate.

This verse is a reference to the establishment of the fourth beast (kingdom). It is a future kingdom, but there are no references as to the beginning of the last kingdom. The final kingdom is the fourth beast that was dreadful and terrible (Dan. 7:7). The final kingdom is also the fourth head and fourth wing on the leopard's back (Dan. 7:6). It is also the fourth horn that sprung up after the goat's one horn was broken (Dan. 8:7–8). The fourth kingdom is synonymous with the ten toes in Nebuchadnezzar's image (Dan. 2:41–42). The fourth kingdom is the kingdom of Thrace, which is known as the eastern kingdom. It is the final world kingdom to dominate Israel, and it is a confederation of ten kings.

The final kingdom will have ten horns. In prophecy, horns are symbolic for a nation or leader of a nation. Soon after the ten kings unite to establish the final kingdom, another horn (king) will rise to power (Dan. 7:7–8). The new king is the little horn that rooted up three of the original horns. The little horn is also synonymous with the little horn that arose from the four horns of the goat (Dan. 8:8–9). This little horn is symbolic for Antichrist. He will be the leader of the final kingdom before the return of Christ. Please note, the final kingdom will be in power before the Antichrist comes on the scene. He will exercise his dominance by uprooting three of the original kings. Confirmation of his dominance is in Daniel. 7:7, 20, 24; and Revelation 12:3; 13:1; and 17:3, 7, 12, 16–17.

At first, the Antichrist will initiate peace; then he will begin to show his true colors. He will be mighty because he has the backing of seven of the original ten kings. He will be a strong leader because he will have sophisticated weaponry. Where weapons cannot tread, he uses other antics and corruptible acts. He will begin by polluting the sanctuary in Jerusalem. He will take away the daily sacrifice (Dan. 9:27) and will erect the abomination of desolation, forcing people into idol worship (Mat. 24:15).

Some scholars say this verse is consistent with Antiochus IV Epiphanes, but he was not a part of the final kingdom. He was in the Syrian kingdom. The Roman Empire succeeded the Syria kingdom, and Antichrist's kingdom is after the Roman kingdom.

> Dan. 11:32   And such as do wickedly against the covenant shall he corrupt by flatteries: but the people that do know their God shall be strong, and do exploits.
>
> Dan. 11:33   And they that understand among the people shall instruct many: yet they shall fall by the sword, and by flame, by captivity, and by spoil, many days.
>
> Dan. 11:34   Now when they shall fall, they shall be holpen with a little help: but many shall cleave to them with flatteries.
>
> Dan. 11:35   And some of them of understanding shall fall, to try them, and to purge, and to make them white, even to the time of the end: because it is yet for a time appointed.

Many of the unrighteous people will succumb to corruption by flattery. They will appear to help others, but in reality, they are deceiving them and helping themselves. The righteous people will continue to be strong in their faith. They will attempt to teach against the Antichrist, but their efforts will fail. Some of them will face execution. Some will endure torture. Others will become slaves.

About this time, the people will begin to experience the Great Tribulation. Although things are bad on earth, it still isn't time for Christ to return. He will return at the time appointed, but no one knows the exact date (Mat. 24:36).

Dan. 11:36   And the king shall do according to his will; and he shall
             exalt himself, and magnify himself above every god, and
             shall speak marvellous things against the God of gods,
             and shall prosper till the indignation be accomplished:
             for that that is determined shall be done.

The Antichrist will do according to his will. He will exalt himself.
He will magnify himself above every god, and he will speak marvelous
things against Almighty God. Revelation 13:6 states, "And he opened his
mouth in blasphemy against God, to blaspheme his name, and his taber-
nacle, and them that dwell in heaven." Second Thessalonians 2:4 states,
"Who opposeth and exalteth himself above all that is called God, or that
is worshipped; so that he as God sitteth in the temple of God, shewing
himself that he is God." Antichrist will continue to prosper until he causes
God's anger to peak.

Dan. 11:37   Neither shall he regard the God of his fathers, nor
             the desire of women, nor regard any god: for he shall
             magnify himself above all.

Antichrist will not worship the God of his fathers. Some scholars
think he is part Hebrew; therefore, the phrase *God of his fathers* is a reference to the Almighty God; the God of Abraham, Isaac, and Jacob. Neither
will he be sympathetic to the desire of women. Some say he is of the
same-sex persuasion, but this passage can also mean that he will not marry
anyone. Others say he does not honor the desire of women because he will
consider himself to be a god named Tammuz (Eze. 8:14). This idea parallels with Antichrist not desiring women because heavenly beings cannot
marry; angels cannot marry; and resurrected saints cannot marry (Mat.
22:30). Antichrist will not regard any god because he will magnify himself
above all gods.

Dan. 11:38   But in his estate shall he honour the God of forces: and

> a god whom his fathers knew not shall he honour with
> gold, and silver, and with precious stones, and pleasant
> things.

Antichrist's power and strength are reflective in his military might, and he is under the supervision of Satan. The phrase, he will honor or worship a god whom his fathers did not know, seems to indicate that he will be of at least partial Hebrew descent. It is possible that he will be a Samaritan because a Samaritan is of mixed race; part Hebrew and part Gentile.[19] The definition of Samaritan parallels with Ezra 10:14–44 because during the Babylonian captivity, some of the Hebrew men took pagan women for their wives.

> Dan. 11:39   Thus shall he do in the most strong holds with a strange
>   god, whom he shall acknowledge and increase with
>   glory: and he shall cause them to rule over many, and
>   shall divide the land for gain.

Antichrist's god will be mystifying. His God is Satan who will increase him with glory. Satan will cause him to rule over many people and cause him to divide the land of Israel for gain. This statement coincides with Revelation 13:2, which states, "And the dragon gave him his power, and his seat, and great authority."

> Dan. 11:40   And at the time of the end shall the king of the south
>   push at him: and the king of the north shall come
>   against him like a whirlwind, with chariots, and with
>   horsemen, and with many ships; and he shall enter into
>   the countries, and shall overflow and pass over.
> Dan. 11:41   He shall enter also into the glorious land, and many
>   countries shall be overthrown: but these shall escape out

---

[19] *The Nelson's New Illustrated Bible Dictionary* (Thomas Nelson Publishers, 1995), 1119.

of his hand, even Edom, and Moab, and the chief of the
children of Ammon.

Dan. 11:42   He shall stretch forth his hand also upon the countries:
and the land of Egypt shall not escape.

Dan. 11:43   But he shall have power over the treasures of gold and
of silver, and over all the precious things of Egypt: and
the Libyans and the Ethiopians shall be at his steps.

During the time of the end of the tribulation period, the king of the
South is not Egypt, and the king of the North is not Syria. The Romans had
previously conquered them. At this point the king of the South is Israel,
and the king of the North is Antichrist, who commands the northern army
that will invade Israel to the south (Eze. 38 and 39). Antichrist will not
conquer the entire world. Edom, Ammon, and Moab are among the names
of a few countries that escape his dominance. These countries are known
as present-day Jordan. Antichrist only conquers twenty-five percent of the
world (Rev. 6:8). He will be powerful spiritually, financially, and politically.
Please note, he accumulates all of his prosperity directly from Satan.

Dan. 11:44   But tidings out of the east and out of the north shall
trouble him: therefore he shall go forth with great fury
to destroy, and utterly to make away many.

Dan. 11:45   And he shall plant the tabernacles of his palace between
the seas in the glorious holy mountain; yet he shall come
to his end, and none shall help him.

Antichrist is the king of the North, and he will receive news or intelligence from the north and east that troubles him. Armed with this news,
he will go forth with great fury to destroy that immediate threat. He will
establish his military perimeter between the seas in the glorious holy mountain. The glorious holy mountain is Mt. Zion, Jerusalem, and the seas are
the Salt (Dead) Sea and the Mediterranean Sea. There, he will be defeated,
and no one will come to his defense.

Some scholars seem to think the Antichrist will originate from a revived Roman Empire. The Roman Empire is the third head and third wing of the leopard (Dan. 7:6) and the third horn of the goat (Dan 8:8). The debut of Antichrist is from the fourth beast that consists of ten horns (ten kings). He will root up three of the original ten horns. Scripture seems to dictate Antichrist will originate from the revived Grecian Empire. When Alexander the Great died, the Grecian kingdom split into four different kingdoms. The Roman Empire was the third of four horns derived from the divided Grecian kingdom. Antichrist's kingdom comes from the fourth horn of the divided Grecian kingdom, of which he assumed leadership by uprooting three of the original ten horns (kings). Antichrist's kingdom is from the revived Grecian kingdom instead of the revived Roman Empire.

CHAPTER 12

HIS RETURN

Dan. 12:1   And at that time shall Michael stand up, the great prince which standeth for the children of thy people: and there shall be a time of trouble, such as never was since there was a nation even to that same time: and at that time thy people shall be delivered, every one that shall be found written in the book.

When Michael Stands Up

THE setting is just prior to the end of the great tribulation period. Christ is preparing for his return. He will return by sending Michael the archangel with the sound of the trumpet (1Th. 4:16). The sounding of the trumpet by Michael is the initiation of the return of Christ, which is the first resurrection (Rev. 20:4–5). Those individuals whose names are written in the Book of Life will experience a transformation of their mortal bodies in the twinkling of an eye (1Co. 15:51–53). When Christ returns, Antichrist will suffer a devastating defeat.

Dan. 12:2   And many of them that sleep in the dust of the earth shall awake, some to everlasting life, and some to shame and everlasting contempt.

It's time for many of those individuals who are dead and buried to receive their resurrection. The text states that some will awaken to everlasting life, and some will awaken to shame and everlasting contempt. The phrase *sleep in the dust* does not necessarily mean all the dead is resurrected.

The word *sleep* can also mean to be slack, and the phrase *in the dust* can also mean live on earth. Therefore those that awaken to shame and contempt are those individuals that are awaken mentally and are now cognizant that they have been wrong about not following Christ. It is too late for them to partake in the first resurrection; their destiny is eternal punishment unless they repent. Some will repent, but others will continue on a path of destruction.

> Dan. 12:3   And they that be wise shall shine as the brightness of the firmament; and they that turn many to righteousness as the stars for ever and ever.

During the tribulation period, many individuals will experience enormous turmoil. Many righteous individuals will shine as the brightness of the sky because they will speak out against the Antichrist and his tactics. They will be responsible for many people realizing the truth and becoming born-again. They will shine like stars because they have illuminated the thinking of many non-believers.

> Dan. 12:4   But thou, O Daniel, shut up the words, and seal the book, even to the time of the end: many shall run to and fro, and knowledge shall be increased.

Daniel receives instructions to stop writing down the things that Gabriel is explaining to him. He was further instructed to stop recording because the information that he is receiving will be manifested many centuries in the future. God gave Daniel a glimpse of the end-times events but commanded that he stop recording it. In the meantime, many people will run to and fro, and their knowledge about the end times will increase as we approach the return of Christ. Years ago humanity did not have the technology that we enjoy today, such as computers, satellites, televisions, and so forth. Today man has enjoyed many technological advances, and his knowledge about interpreting the end-time events has increased exponentially.

Dan. 12:5   Then I Daniel looked, and, behold, there stood other two, the one on this side of the bank of the river, and the other on that side of the bank of the river.

Dan. 12:6   And one said to the man clothed in linen, which was upon the waters of the river, How long shall it be to the end of these wonders?

Dan. 12:7   And I heard the man clothed in linen, which was upon the waters of the river, when he held up his right hand and his left hand unto heaven, and sware by him that liveth for ever that it shall be for a time, times, and an half; and when he shall have accomplished to scatter the power of the holy people, all these things shall be finished.

Daniel looked up from his writings, and he saw two other heavenly beings standing by the river. One stood on this side of the river, and the other stood on the other bank of the river. The name of this river is the Hiddekel River (Dan. 10:4). Another name for the Hiddekel River is the Tigris River.

One of the heavenly beings asked the man that was clothed in linen a question. The man clothed in linen is Gabriel, but scripture does not identify the other two men. It is Gabriel that is explaining everything to Daniel. The question he asked is, "How long shall it be to the end of these wonders?" The great tribulation is the "wonders" the heavenly being was referencing.

Gabriel's responded by holding up his hands to heaven and swearing that it will last for a time and times and a half of time. *A Time* is one year, *times* is two years, and *half a time* is one-half year; therefore, the great tribulation will last for three and one-half years. It will take three and a half years before Antichrist can successfully manage to diminish the will of God's people. If the Lord does not intervene, then Antichrist could potentially destroy every individual on earth (Mat. 24:21–22).

Dan. 12:8   And I heard, but I understood not: then said I, O my
             Lord, what shall be the end of these things?

Daniel heard the answer that Gabriel gave the heavenly being about
how long the Great Tribulation would last. He did not fully comprehend
its meaning, so he took it upon himself to ask Gabriel what would happen
at the end of the great tribulation.

Dan. 12:9   And he said, Go thy way, Daniel: for the words are
             closed up and sealed till the time of the end.
Dan. 12:10   Many shall be purified, and made white, and tried; but
             the wicked shall do wickedly: and none of the wicked
             shall understand; but the wise shall understand.

Gabriel responded to Daniel and told him not to be too concerned
about the end of the tribulation because the meaning is secret. That information will remain sealed until the end-times are upon us. He proceeded to
tell him that during the great tribulation, many will begin to examine themselves. Some will repent and become born again. Still, others will continue
to live their same old lifestyle. Those who are wise will understand the
events that are happening during the great tribulation, but the nefarious
and diabolical ones are oblivious to the fact that Christ is preparing to
return.

Please note, Daniel was instructed to seal up the writings. Perhaps the
words that Daniel was ordered to seal at the behest of Gabriel is the book
with seven seals that John saw in the book of Revelation (Rev. 5:1).

Dan. 12:11   And from the time that the daily sacrifice shall be taken
             away, and the abomination that maketh desolate set up,
             there shall be a thousand two hundred and ninety days.
Dan. 12:12   Blessed is he that waiteth, and cometh to the thousand
             three hundred and five and thirty days.

From the time that the daily sacrifice is jeopardized, and the abomination of desolation installed, a thousand and two hundred and ninety days will pass. Those who endure until the 1,335th day are going to be blessed. The daily sacrifice is the ritual of daily prayer. It will cease in the middle of a seven-year covenant that Antichrist ratifies with Israel (Dan. 9:27). When Antichrist thwarts the daily sacrifice, Israel will no longer be allowed to offer their prayers to the Lord and worship freely.

The abomination of desolation is an image that is strategically placed in Jerusalem at their place of worship (Mat. 24:15). From the announcement that the daily sacrifice is to cease until the abomination of desolation (image) is erected, approximately forty-five days will pass. The abomination of desolation is an image of Antichrist, and he claims that he is their god. Once the abomination of desolation is in position and fully operational, it will begin to speak. It will demand that the people bow down and worship the image as the only god of the universe.

Jesus instructed the people of Jerusalem to flee into the mountains when they see the abomination of desolation (Mat. 24:15–16). The dedication of the abomination of desolation is the beginning of great tribulation (Mat. 24:15–21). The flight from Jerusalem to the mountains after the abomination of desolation is in position will take approximately thirty days.

The amount of time the people will spend in the wilderness is predetermined. It will be for 1,260 days (Rev. 12:6). Revelation 12:14 describes the time spent in the wilderness as *a time* (one year), *times* (two years), and *half a time* (one-half year). The total time they are destined to reside in the wilderness is three and one-half years.

As soon as the abomination of desolation is in position, the people begin to flee from Jerusalem into the wilderness, and it take them thirty days to reach the wilderness. Once they reach the wilderness, they are going to spend 1,260 days there, under the protection of God. That's 1,290 days total.

Antichrist will announce his intentions to stop the daily sacrifice, but it will not end with the announcement. It will take another forty-five days before the abomination of desolation can be constructed. Once it is strategically positioned in Jerusalem, the people of Jerusalem will flee to the wilderness.

Event	Days
Daily sacrifice prohibition announced	---
Abomination of Desolation installed	45
Jerusalem fleeing into the wilderness	30
Survivors protected in the wilderness	1260
Total	**1,335 days**

There will be 2,300 days set aside for the prohibition of the daily sacrifice and the installation of the abomination of desolation (Dan. 8:13–14). Please note, the ritual of the daily sacrifice (prayer) was mandated twice daily. That being the case, the 2,300 times that the daily sacrifice is forbidden is only 1,150 days. Once the implementation of the abomination of desolation and the prohibition of the daily sacrifice are in place, it continues right up to the minute that Antichrist faces his destruction.

To get a clearer picture of the time frame, we have to count backward. The 2,300 mornings and evening sacrifices total 1,150 days. That means that the enforcement of the prohibition of the daily sacrifice began on the 1,370 day of the seven-year covenant. There are 1,290 days once the abomination of desolation is introduced (Dan. 12:11). That seems to cause a contradiction. Perhaps the abomination of desolation was strategically positioned but not fully operational until sometime later. Perhaps the dedication ceremony will take place 140 days after it is initially positioned in the Holy Place. The 140 days plus the 1,150 days will account for the 1,290 days from the time that the abomination is visibly standing in the Holy Place. See Appendix H for more detail.

Here is the timeline to all the events concerning the seven-year covenant between Antichrist and Israel. The day that it is approved and ratified is the beginning of the week (seven-year period). That day is day number zero. In biblical terms, each year consists of 360 days; therefore seven years is a total of 2,520 days.

On day 1,185 of the covenant, Antichrist violates it by announcing that the daily sacrifice will be prohibited. Immediately after the announcement of the prohibition of the daily sacrifice, the preparation of the abomination of desolation begins, perhaps in a warehouse somewhere in Jerusalem. It takes forty-five days to complete the construction, which brings us to day 1,230 of the covenant. Day 1,230 is the day that the abomination of desolation is in position in the Holy Place. It is visible by the citizens of Jerusalem. Day 1,230 is also the day that Jesus referenced when he instructed the people to flee into the wilderness when they see the abomination of desolation standing in the Holy Place (Mat. 24:15).

On day 1,230 of the covenant, the citizens of Jerusalem will visibly see the abomination placed in the Holy Place; therefore, they will begin to flee from the city of Jerusalem. Once the citizens began to flee Jerusalem, Antichrist will send his army to stop them (Rev. 12:13–14). The Lord will see that Antichrist's army is fast approaching the fleeing citizens of Jerusalem, so he helps them escape the pursuing army by causing an earthquake to swallow up the majority of that army (Rev. 12:16).

It takes the fleeing citizens of Jerusalem thirty days to reach the wilderness. They arrive in the wilderness on day 1,260 of the covenant. The citizens of Jerusalem receive protection in the wilderness for 1,260 days (Rev. 12:6). One thousand two hundred and sixty days after their arrival in the wilderness brings us to day 2,520, which is the end of the seven-year covenant and the destruction of Antichrist.

Once the remainder of the army that wasn't swallowed in the earthquake realized that have been outmaneuvered, they return to Jerusalem and begin to make preparation to enforce the prohibition of the daily sacrifice. Around this time is the implementation of the mark of the Beast. During this time, praise and worship of Almighty God is prohibited, and buying and selling will also be restricted. This time frame is known as the great tribulation. This is the worst tribulation that has ever overshadowed the earth (Mat. 24:21).

The daily sacrifice will last in its entirety for 2,300 days (Dan. 8:13–14). All of these days and time might seem a bit confusing because Daniel 12:11 implies it will last 1,290 days. Note, the text mentions the prohibition of the daily sacrifice and the transgression that "makes desolate." These are two different things. The daily sacrifice is daily prayer and prohibiting a person from praying in an open setting is not a sin that leads to damnation. It does not promote a healthy praise and worship environment but is not damnable. One can still pray and worship in silence and secret. The transgression of desolation is a challenge that once accepted and consummated, one has committed the unpardonable sin and has entered into a state of eternal damnation.

Is there a transgression that is associated with the daily prayer that will cause eternal damnation? Revelation 14:9–11 states, "If any man worship the beast and his image, and receive his mark in his forehead, or in his hand, The same shall drink of the wine of the wrath of God, which is poured out without mixture into the cup of his indignation; and he shall be tormented with fire and brimstone in the presence of the holy angels, and in the presence of the Lamb: And the smoke of their torment ascendeth up for ever and ever: and they have no rest day nor night, who worship the beast and his image, and whosoever receiveth the mark of his name." Accepting the mark of the Beast or worshipping his image is committing the unpardonable sin.

The abomination of desolation is an idol or an image that is a replica of the beast or Antichrist (Rev. 13:14). Worshipping the beast is equivalent to accepting the beast as Almighty God. Not only does worshipping the beast or his image initiate eternal damnation, but having his mark as an identification tattooed on one's body is also acceptance of a false god and rejection of Almighty God. The abomination of desolation is the image of the beast (Antichrist). The image is harmless until the moment one worships it or voluntarily accepts its mark.

The ritual of daily prayer and worship was done twice daily; therefore, individuals will have the opportunity to worship the mark of the Beast 2300 times or 1150 days. The mark of the Beast is only available to be accepted during the final 1,150 days of the seven-year covenant. The implementation of the mark of the Beast is established on day 1,370 of the covenant, which is 140 days after the abomination of desolation is first spotted in the Holy Place. Please note, having the abomination of desolation (an idol) in your presence is not a transgression of the law. The transgression of desolation is worshipping the abomination of desolation or accepting its mark. The mark is better known as the mark of the Beast, and it will last for approximately three years and two months after its implementation. Acceptance of the mark of the Beast is a willful, wicked, and abominable act, and the consequences are eternal damnation.

> Dan. 12:13   But go thou thy way till the end be: for thou shalt rest, and stand in thy lot at the end of the days.

Daniel is instructed to stop writing and seal any further interpretations of the visions, dreams, and revelations he experienced in the Babylonian and Medo-Persian kingdoms. All of these events are future, and much of it will be during the end-times. By this time, Daniel is an old man. Gabriel informed Daniel that he would not physically live to see the fulfillment of all of these events, but he will receive his rewards when all of these events come to complete fruition.

APPENDICES

APPENDIX A

CHRONOLOGICAL ORDER OF THE BOOK OF DANIEL

Chapter	King	Year	Event
Chapter 1	Jehoiakim	3rd year	Victory over Judah
Chapter 2	Nebuchadnezzar	2nd year	Dream of Great Image
Chapter 3	Nebuchadnezzar		Image of Gold/Fiery Furnace
Chapter 4	Nebuchadnezzar		Mentality of an Animal
Chapter 10	Cyrus	3rd year	Gabriel appears to Daniel
Chapter 7	Belshazzar	1st year	Vision of Four Beasts
Chapter 8	Belshazzar	3rd year	Vision of the Ram and Goat
Chapter 5	Belshazzar	Last year	Handwriting on the Wall
Chapter 6	Darius	1st year	Daniel in the Lion's Den
Chapter 9	Darius	1st year	Daniel's Seventy Weeks
Chapter 11	Darius	1st year	Gabriel divulges interpretation
Chapter 12	Darius	1st year	Continuation of interpretation

APPENDIX B

CHRONOLOGICAL ORDER OF THE KINGS

King	Country	Scripture
King Jehoiakim	Judah	Dan. 1:1
King Nebuchadnezzar	Babylon	Dan. 1:1
King Cyrus	Persia	Dan. 10:1
King Belshazzar	Babylon	Dan. 7:1
King Darius	Medes	Dan. 9:1

APPENDIX C

NAME CHANGES

Old Name	Old Name Meaning	New Name	New Name Meaning
Daniel	God Is my Judge	Belteshazzar	Treasure of Bel
Hananiah	God Has Favored	Shadrach	Friend of the King
Mishael	Who Is or What God Is	Meshach	God of Sheshach
Azariah	God Has Helped	Abednego	Servant of Nebo

Appendix D

Animal References

Lion
Bear
Leopard
Fourth beast
Ram with two horns
Goat with one horn

APPENDIX E

WORLD KINGDOMS

Babylonian
Medo-Persian
Grecian
Syrian
Egyptian
Roman
Babylonian/Antichrist

APPENDIX F

NEBUCHADNEZZAR'S DREAMS

KING Nebuchadnezzar dreamed of a great image. The different body parts of the image were constructed of different metals. The different metals represent different kingdoms.

He also had another dream about a great tree that reaches into heaven. The tree was hewn down, and the stump that was left was fitted with a brass band and an iron band. The references to the different stages of the tree are also symbolisms for different kingdoms.

Body Parts	Metal	Identifying Traits	Sequence	Kingdom
Head	Gold	Tree	1st kingdom	Babylon
Arms and Breast	Silver	Stump	2nd kingdom	Medo-Persian
Belly and Thighs	Brass	Brass Band	3rd kingdom	Grecian
1st Leg	Iron	Iron Band	4th kingdom	Syrian
2nd Leg	Iron	Iron Band	5th kingdom	Egyptian
Two Feet	Iron/Clay	Iron Band	6th kingdom	Roman
Ten Toes	Iron/Clay	Iron Band	7th kingdom	Antichrist

Appendix G

Symbolisms

Symbols	Meaning	Identification	Kingdoms
Image	World Kingdoms		
Tree	Kingdom		
Heads	Kingdoms		
Horns	Kings		
Wings	Reign of Kingdom		
Lion	1st Kingdom		Babylonian
	2 wings—reign of:	Nebuchadnezzar Belshazzar	
Bear	2nd Kingdom		Medo-Persian
	3 Ribs	Babylon/Medes/ Persia	
Ram	2nd Kingdom		Medo-Persian
	2 Horns	Medes/Persians	
Goat	3rd Kingdom		Grecian
	Goat with 1 Horn	Alexander the Great	
	Goat's Horn broken	Fall of Grecian Kingdom	
	4 new Horns are Born	Rise of 4 lesser Kingdoms	
	1st Horn	1st lesser Kingdom	Syrian
	2nd Horn	2nd lesser Kingdom	Egyptian
	3rd Horn	3rd lesser Kingdom	Roman
	4th Horn	4th lesser Kingdom	Babylonian
	Little Horn	Antichrist	Babylonian
Leopard	3rd Kingdom		Grecian
	4 Heads	4 lesser Kingdoms	
	4 Wings	Reign of 4 lesser Kingdoms	

		1st Head/1st Wing	Syrian
		2nd Head/2nd Wing	Egyptian
		3rd Head/3rd Wing	Roman
4th Beast	4th Kingdom/4th Horn	4th Head/4th Wing	Babylonian
	10 horns	4th Head/4th Wing	Babylonian
	Little Horn	Antichrist	Babylonian

Appendix H

Week 70

7-year Covenant Ratified
Beginning of the Week

Antichrist violates the Covenant

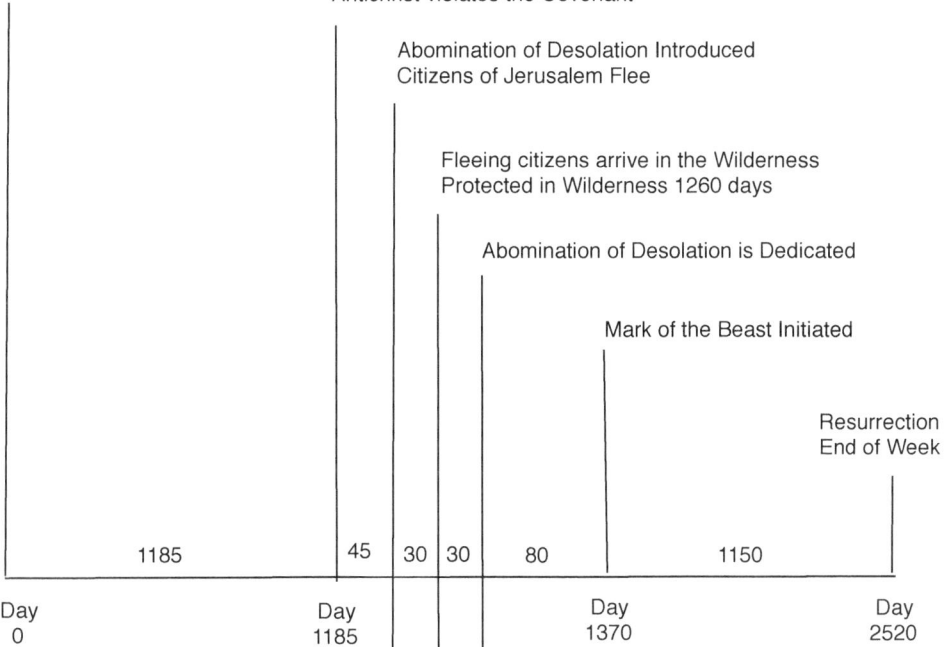

Abomination of Desolation Introduced
Citizens of Jerusalem Flee

Fleeing citizens arrive in the Wilderness
Protected in Wilderness 1260 days

Abomination of Desolation is Dedicated

Mark of the Beast Initiated

Resurrection
End of Week

| 1185 | 45 | 30 | 30 | 80 | 1150 |

Day
0

Day
1185

Day
1370

Day
2520

Day
1230

Day
1260

Day
1290

1 week = 7 years

1 year = 360 days

7 years = 2520 days

Day 1185 is approximately 3 yrs. 3 mo. 15 da.
Day 1230 is approximately 3 yrs. 5 mo.
Day 1260 is approximately 3 yrs. 6 mo.
Day 1290 is approximately 3 yrs. 7 mo.
Day 1370 is approximately 3 yrs. 9 mo. 20 da.

Duration of the Mark of the Beast
Approximately 3 yrs. 2 mo. 10 da.

APPENDIX I

DREAMS/VISIONS

Images	Metals	Kingdoms	Sequence	Beasts	Wings	Heads	Other	Horns
Head	Gold	Babylon	1st	Lion	2 wings Nebuchadnezzar Belshazzar		Tree	
Arms Breasts	Silver	Medo- Persian	2nd	Bear	3 ribs Medes/Persia Babylon		Ram Stump	2 horns 1 taller Both broken
Belly Thighs	Brass	Grecian	3rd	Leopard	4 wings	4 heads	Goat Brass Band	1 horn broken 4 replaced it
Legs	Iron	**Third Beast is further divided into four other remnants**						
1st leg	Iron	Syrian	4th		1st wing	1st head		
2nd leg	Iron	Egyptian	5th		2nd wing	2nd head		
2 feet	Iron Clay	Roman	6th		3rd wing	3rd head		
10 toes	Iron Clay	Final	7th	Fourth Beast	4th wing	4th head	Iron Band	10
Fourth Beast (Kingdom) undergoes Leadership Change								
10 toes	Iron Clay	Babylonian Antichrist	7th	Dreadful Terrible	4th wing	4th head		10 + 1 − 3 = 8 Little Horn

www.ingramcontent.com/pod-product-compliance
Lightning Source LLC
LaVergne TN
LVHW051639080426
835511LV00016B/2395